Asking Better Questions

NORAH MORGAN

JULIANA SAXTON

2nd Edition

Pembroke Publishers Limited

To Charles Morgan and
Christopher Saxton
whose being made the
Unanswerable questions
easier to endure

© 2006 Pembroke Publishers
   538 Hood Road
   Markham, Ontario, Canada L3R 3K9
   www.pembrokepublishers.com

Distributed in the U.S. by Stenhouse Publishers
480 Congress Street
Portland, ME 04101-3400
www.stenhouse.com

We acknowledge the financial support of the Government of Canada through
the Book Publishing Industry Development Program (BPIDP) for our publishing activities.

We acknowledge the assistance of the OMDC Book Fund, an initiative of the
Ontario Media Development Corporation.

Library and Archives Canada Cataloguing in Publication

Morgan, Norah
   Asking better questions / Norah Morgan, Juliana Saxton. — 2nd ed.

Includes bibliographical references and index.
ISBN 13: 978-1-55138-209-8
ISBN 10: 1-55138-209-1

   1. Questioning. 2. Teaching. 3. Learning. I. Saxton, Juliana
II. Title.

LB1027.44.M67 2006   371.102   C2006-904811-8

Editor: Kate Revington
Cover design: John Zehethofer
Typesetting: Jay Tee Graphics

Printed and bound in Canada
9 8 7 6 5 4 3 2

Contents

Acknowledgments *6*
Foreword by John O'Toole *7*
Introduction: Questioning as a Democratic Skill *9*

1 What Seems to Be the Problem? *13*

How do we view the student in the educational process? *15*
What is a vigorous learner? *16*

2 A Question of Thinking *18*

So, what is thinking? *19*
"Where is the boy . . . ?": Kinds of thinking *20*
1. Questions that draw upon knowledge (Remembering) *20*
2. Questions that test comprehension (Understanding) *21*
3. Questions that require application (Solving) *22*
4. Questions that encourage analysis (Reasoning) *22*
5. Questions that invite synthesis (Creating) *23*
6. Questions that promote evaluation (Judging) *24*
Reflecting on Bloom and Little Boy Blue *24*

3 A Question of Feeling *27*

The Taxonomy of Personal Engagement *27*
Interest *28*
Engaging *29*
Committing *29*
Internalizing *29*
Interpreting *30*
Evaluating *31*
Ownership through deepening engagement *31*
The role of the taxonomy in questioning *31*

4 The Example Lesson: Snow White *34*

The lesson plan *34*
The lesson: What actually happened *36*
Reflections on the use of two taxonomies *44*

5 A Classification of Questions *45*

A classification of questions by general function *45*
Category A: Eliciting information—On the line *46*
Category B: Shaping understanding—Between the lines *48*
Category C: Pressing for reflection—Beyond the lines *51*
Flexible, non-hierarchical use of questions *54*

6 The Example Lesson: Finding Areas *55*

Session 1: Is there room for a football field? *55*
Session 2: Why does a farmer need to calculate areas? *58*
Session 3: How can settlers ensure that land is divided fairly? *59*
Reflections on the lesson *61*

7 A Glossary of Questions *63*

From higher-order to unanswerable questions *63*
Alternatives to questions *72*
What's in a name? *73*

8 Fewer Questions, Better Questions, and Time to Think *74*

Classroom discourse—Talking in wide circles *74*
Characteristics of effective classroom discourse *75*
Characteristics of a good question *77*
Characteristics of an active responding process *78*
Why do teachers ask so many questions? *79*
Thinking time *80*

9 Putting the Question, Handling the Answer *82*

General teaching requirements *82*
General teaching techniques *83*
Distribution, or targeting, of questions *85*
Reinforcing for success *87*
Probing for deeper thought *89*
When *not* to ask a question *90*
Dealing with answers *91*
Responding to answers: Some things to avoid *93*

10 The Case for the Student as Questioner *99*

Why aren't more questions coming from students? *100*
Addressing the pressures against the teaching of questioning skills *100*
Teaching in ways that promote responsibility for learning *105*

11 Switching Places: The Student as Questioner *107*

Modelling how to question *107*
Overt ways to model questions *108*
Training and practice in questioning *109*

12 The Example Lesson: Ann Graham *119*

Session 1: Raising questions *119*
Session 2: Building a story through questioning *122*
Session 3: Writing based on information gathered *126*
Session 4: Examining how questions helped build the story *127*
Raising difficult questions *128*

Appendixes

1: Differences between social talk, classroom discourse and
   discussion   *130*
2: Who asks questions?   *132*
3: Building questions upon questions   *134*
4: Thinking as someone else   *136*
5: Evaluating questions on Ann Graham   *139*
6: Questioning behaviors   *141*
7: Changing perspectives in the classroom   *142*
8: Getting started: A thinking process for teachers   *145*

Bibliography   *149*
Index   *155*
Postscript   *159*

Acknowledgments

We are especially grateful to the following colleagues: Cecily O'Neill and Margaret Burke who read the earliest drafts and made some startlingly sensible suggestions which put us on the right track; Ida McCann, teaching and learning project officer, for her invitation to work with the Tasmanian teachers whose enthusiasm and insights got us started in the first place; to Madge Craig and Vicki Green for sharing their research and classroom expertise; and to Dr. Frances Halpenny for her invaluable assistance at a critical moment. We thank all those who invited us to give workshops following the publication of the first edition. We learned so much from participants who shared their experiences. And to Barbara Hill who used her classroom experience to make this new edition more teacher-worthy, we owe a standing ovation.

We are grateful to the following for permission to quote material: the *Toronto Star* syndicate for an extract from "Temagami" by Kathleen Kenna (8 December 1988); McClelland & Stewart Publishers, courtesy of the Lucinda Vardey Agency and A. P. Watt Literary Agents (on behalf of the estate of Margaret Laurence) for an extract from *A Bird in the House* by Margaret Laurence; Random House Inc. (© 1987 James A. Michener) for an extract from *Legacy* by James A. Michener; and William Stafford, whose poem "Traveling through the Dark" appears in *Stories That Could Be True*, published by Harper & Row (1977).

We are indebted to Jonothan Neelands, Paul Bidwell, Carole Tarlington, and Linda Laidlaw for allowing us to make use of their teaching structures; and to our students and colleagues who let us test out the work on them and never hesitated to refine and reshape our theory and practice with grace and humor. Joanne Smith and Kim Pelchat at the Resource Centre, Faculty of Education, Brock University, were infinitely helpful in answering our questions and asking others that we didn't know we needed to ask, and Alexander Saxton appeared at the right moment to help with the boring bits.

Special thanks to Mary Macchiusi, who took on *Teaching, Questioning and Learning* from Routledge and turned it into *Asking Better Questions*. She has prodded and patiently waited for us to prepare this second edition. Thanks, too, to Kate Revington, whose supportive editing has been done with clarity, grace, and style. Above all, we thank Ted Morgan who undertook the nurture and care of authors and refined the art to a degree of perfection hitherto unknown. What heights can yet remain?

Foreword by John O'Toole

When preparing to write this foreword, I reached for my well-thumbed copy of the first edition and realized that an opportunistic student had recently "borrowed it" and departed with it for another continent. My closest colleague has had her copy similarly liberated, also quite recently. And the three copies in our library are all out on loan.

A question schooled by that book rose into my mind—Why? The obvious answer immediately both cooled my resentment, and—as good questions do—generated more and deeper questions: Do the thieves perhaps need it more than we do? What is it about that now elderly book which makes it so sought after by contemporary teachers? Has *Asking Better Questions* changed other people's practices as much as it has mine? How many school principals have read it and encouraged their colleagues to use it? What might happen if a Minister for Education read it and acted on its implications? And of course: Why isn't it compulsory reading for all teachers?

The educational and democratic vision of this brilliant re-write of that truly seminal teaching text goes even higher. In the introduction, the authors spell out clearly that effective questioning is the key to responsible, active, resourceful, democratic citizenship. Moreover, it is also the crucial link between our agency as those responsible citizens and how we and our children are schooled in classrooms, where often the opposite still holds sway—dependency and oppression: "You're not here to ask questions, you're here to listen to me and learn" (verbatim as I overheard not so long ago from a colleague leading a teacher education class). Of course, any good teacher knows that an effective classroom is a place of dialogue, not monologue, and that the teacher's job is to maximize the possibilities of that dialogue. This means, first of all, the ability to ask the right questions: those that generate, sustain, and deepen dialogue; equally important, it means the skill to help the students ask the right questions, too, and go on asking them. As the authors wisely point out, knowing what the right question is at any time and having the humility to trust the respondent to answer it productively rather than necessarily "correctly" are real skills, or actually a broad range of skills, that demand practice, training, and experience … and this book.

The authors show vividly how these skills are not just cognitive, but deeply affective. To be an effective questioner, the teacher cannot just transport the brain and a set of procedures into the classroom like a data stick and leave the senses and sensibilities at the door. Empathy, not just sympathy, is one of the vital ingredients of that sensibility, helping students to step into others' shoes and questioning how those others feel and why they act that way, discovering multiple perspectives and viewpoints that raise further questions, and helping us to see the complexity of our lives as humans.

For me, it has been a great privilege for over twenty years to have known and occasionally worked with the late Norah Morgan and the very live Juliana Saxton, surely the most productive double act in the fields of both drama education and transformative, reflective pedagogy. Not easy, though: they have always known fearlessly how to interrogate, to ask the disconcerting question that rocks the smug confidence of certainty ... but invites us to take up the challenge, to find the model that works, the idea that gels, the question that will impel us forward. The authors are uncompromisingly practical and equally scholarly. That's partly what makes this book so engaging: their praxis is absolutely rooted in real classrooms and real students, and the book is a cornucopia of vivid and useable examples, seen through the eyes of both the teachers and the students with great sympathy and tough love. The book is equally well rooted in tough, critical reflection and research, examining and, yes, questioning all the examples and the practice.

I hope the readers will enjoy as much as I do the ingenious device of using a sidebar to provide two quite contrasting components—helpful logistical details about managing the classroom practice being described, juxtaposed with quotations from a wide range of wise voices, challenging, inspiring, and sometimes startling. This sidebar conversation disrupts, but does not distract from the main text. Cunningly, it keeps alive the sense that this book (which is a basically monological form) is itself a dialogue ... and keeps us asking questions.

I hope, too, that the publishers manage to get this book to an audience as big as it deserves—namely, all teachers. Morgan and Saxton have long ago achieved legendary status among the small, growing, and robust band of educators exploring the liberatory, transformative opportunities of experiential dramatic pedagogy. Though not among the band's most vociferous advocates for radical pedagogy, their work has quietly and unerringly mapped it for our twenty-first century, from maths to literacy, from history to ... to what?...

Well, what? And how have they done it? How does it work? And can I do it?

Reader, enquire within.

John O'Toole
Foundation Chair of Arts Education
The University of Melbourne

September 2006

Introduction   Questioning as a Democratic Skill

Nothing is more terrifying to . . . people than someone who thinks in public—that is, someone who questions himself openly. The public itself has been soothed to such an extent by scripted debates imbued with theoretically "right" answers, that it no longer seems to respond positively to arguments which create doubt. Real doubt creates real fear.
—John Ralston Saul (1993, p. 534)

. . . perhaps political leaders everywhere would prefer that the majority of our young people not engage in critical thinking and remain ignorant of these matters. This preference is one that seems to have endured for centuries.
—Nel Noddings (2004, p. 494)

In any nation that works under a democratic system, it is understood that the power rests with its citizens. Elected representation and government are the responsibility of every member of society and each individual is responsible for monitoring the operation of government and for changing that representation when it no longer meets the needs of that society.

In a democracy, the voices of minorities have as much right as the voice of the majority. For both, that right carries with it responsibilities: to see the issues clearly; to cut away the rhetoric and seductions of short-term advantages and to understand the implications; to give expression to concern through constructive action; and to be able to mediate individual concerns within the collective vision.

These responsibilities depend upon the skill of every member of society to ask questions: What is this really about? Whose values are being addressed? Who or what will benefit? Who or what will be diminished? What actions are possible? What am I prepared to give up? The ability and the courage to ask such questions lie at the core of the democratic process.

In *The Unconscious Civilization*, John Ralston Saul (1995) writes that a "citizen-based democracy is built upon participation" (p. 195), and participation, he points out, is "the very expression of permanent discomfort." He is not talking about a physical discomfort but a mental attitude that recognizes and accepts the "tension of uncertainty," that will not allow us to be lulled into passivity and acceptance, into the attitude of mind "What can I do about it? I'm only one person. I have no power to change anything." Saul's "unease" is the kind of "unease that wards off complacency and compliance, that . . . awaken[s] people enough to move them to act" (Greene, 2006, p. 596). For Saul, "the acceptance of psychic discomfort is the acceptance of consciousness." To be conscious is to be alive; alive to oneself, to others and to what is going on in the world; prepared to do something whenever "what is going on" is seen as counter to the good of the whole—not one's *own* good, but the good of the whole.

To be alive to ourselves can be painful! It requires us to have a clear understanding of who we are and what are our wishes, needs, and dreams and the personal history and ethics that created them. To be aware of what is going on and to question that is destabilizing. Doubt can be frightening, as Saul suggests, but learning to question and consider answers helps us tolerate the ambiguities of this infinitely complex world that we inhabit. It is only when we understand our own narratives, writes Jerome Bruner (1996, p. 42), that we can truly begin to develop a responsible sense of self. Being alive to others demands the exercise, not just of sympathy but of that much more difficult quality —difficult because it is active rather than passive—the act of empathy. We need to be able to place ourselves in others' shoes and know from our own experience what another could be feeling and thinking. It is an essential characteristic of the human condition, demanding a generosity of imagination. It is also often very painful because it means mediating personal needs for the good of others.

A responsible sense of self, allied to a sense of the larger society and commitment to the common good, is not all that is required. Taking action—the participatory, observable part of citizenship—requires the exercise of what Saul describes as "the rights of the citizen": to criticize and to reject conformity, passivity, and inevitability. These rights demand the ability to think and opportunities to express that thinking in the social context; to acquire habits of thought that go beyond thinking *about* to thinking *why* and thinking *what if*; to see democracy as an "open possibility" (Greene, 2006). We need to be able to construct in the mind edifices of thought that enable us to see the history and possibility of things. Only then is it possible to discover the questions and create the solutions, to have the courage (and the language) to express that thinking, to risk going against the grain of popular opinion or the authority of the power structure; to stand up for ideas when others are busy blending in. Only with practice in thinking can we come to the understanding that what some may see as the inevitable is as much a human construct as anything else that humans do and is, therefore, equally open to question. The practice of citizenship within a democratic society has *always* to be negotiated.

Negotiation involves citizens in compromise. Compromise requires flexibility and, because there are many right answers, there are always ambiguities and complexities that we have to live with, as well as doubts that the choices we make may, in the end, turn out to be wrong. But think of the exercise of democracy in the civil rights movement; the resistance to the Vietnam War; the ongoing resistance in Canada to the clear cutting of forests and the selling off of water resources. Citizenship, writes Saul, is not about minding your own business. It is not an "easy style of life, but it is perhaps the citizen's primary weapon in the exercise of his or her legitimacy" (1995, p. 169). Becoming a citizen is not easy, and acting as one requires a great deal of practice.

The words Saul uses to describe what is involved in being a good citizen are words that we recognize as components of the *hidden* curriculum—the courage to risk, to question, to think deeply—the habits of mind and personal dispositions in which skills and knowledge, in a wholistic education, are embedded.

We must be aware of this hidden curriculum. We are in danger of producing a generation of young people who have lost the art of conversation, who have lost self-motivation, who see their lives valuable only in response to an external reward system that they did not set up, and who have discovered that taking time to think about, to question, to fail, to move around an issue and see it from different points of view is not valued. If we allow ourselves to bend to political expediencies and directives that have little or nothing to do with what we know to be education, then our culture will be changed and our ideas of democracy will shift significantly (Miller and Saxton, 2004a, p. 41).

A democratic society requires that citizens recognize their common interests and that they fully and openly discuss issues related to common priorities.
—Joseph Kahne and Ellen Middaugh (2006, p. 601)

Habits of Mind

- The ability to imagine new possibilities
- The ability to develop theories that predict the consequences of actions
- The ability to explore relationships from multiple perspectives
- The ability to explore ideas, meaning and emotion through multiple forms
- The ability to reflect upon, assess and adjust behaviour
- The ability to sustain coherent collaborative action
- A generosity of spirit; to be forgiving of mistakes through recognizing that the process is long-term rather than immediate
- The ability to elaborate detail with infinite patience

Personal Dispositions

- Persistence and resilience
- Risk-taking
- Focus and discipline
- Respect for authentic achievement; a reluctance to accept "junk"
- A great sense of joy in the challenges; a delicious sense of achievement in the effective completion of the task

—Richard Deasy (2001)

The classroom has been described as the cradle of democracy and the teacher as one of the most influential nurturers of the democratic process. We know that questioning is the means by which teachers help students to construct meaning. We also know that the collective construction of action that gives voice to that meaning is dependent upon students" skills in *asking* productive questions. This book is offered in the hope that, by examining how to question, we may arrive at answers that will generate richer classroom interactions and provide our students with opportunities to develop and practise that essential democratic skill.

About this book

This book is intended to help teachers understand why questions are so important to teaching and learning in the 21st century. It examines why many teachers are insecure as questioners and why students are so often shut out of the questioning process. It suggests an uncomplicated way to classify the questions that teachers need to ask in order to acquire information, build understanding, and generate reflection. Finally, it offers models, techniques, activities, and examples that promote better questioning by teachers and students.

The ability to question inside the "action" is part of the technique of teacher response that Philip Taylor calls "Reflection-in-action" and is essential to becoming an effective teacher.
—Betty Jane Wagner (1998, pp. 215–216)

The first section of the book examines the two structures that form the matrix of all educational processes: (1) the structure for thinking and (2) the structure for feeling. Until almost the end of the last century, these two operations were seen as separate. Rationality and objectivity have been and still are regarded as characteristics of higher intelligence even though neither is completely possible simply because we are human beings. Feeling is indispensable to effective thinking. Understanding how these structures work will enable you to use them as guides both to evaluate what *has* happened in your classroom and to plan what you *would like to* happen. Most important, they help you understand what is happening *as it is happening*. This, of course, has particular implications for questioning. Although you can and should plan one or two questions, part of effective questioning techniques is to ask the *appropriate* question at the right moment *inside* the give-and-take of classroom talk and activity.

The middle section looks at a simple three-part classification of general functions for questions: questions that tap into what is already known and that elicit a sense of responsibility towards the conduct of and approach to the work; questions that build a context for shared understanding; and questions that challenge students to think critically and creatively. Within this classification, there are many kinds of questions that we present as a glossary so that you may see the wide potential of questions for generating thought and feeling.

This is not a linear text that builds its arguments sequentially. You may, of course, begin at the beginning and work your way through to the end, but you might prefer to leaf through and start where something catches your eye. Whatever focuses your attention can provide an entry point from which you may move back and forth through the text as your interests and needs dictate. Wherever possible, we have talked about teachers and students, but there are times when we talk about *a* teacher and *a* student. We follow the principle that the teacher will be referred to as "she" and the student as "he," unless a specific example dictates the gender.

In the final section of the book, we concentrate on building questioning skills for teacher and students, suggesting techniques for posing questions and dealing with answers. We offer a variety of teaching stances for questions and for answers that will elevate language and encourage divergent thinking. We suggest roles and situations that will engage students as questioners and as answerers, and we provide practical exercises for developing these skills.

Each of the three sections is illustrated with an example lesson, drawn from our own experience or those of our colleagues and students.

Although some things have been synthesized for clarity and brevity, everything described throughout the text has been test-driven in the real world of the classroom.

Beyond the three main parts of the book, this new edition features activities to help you clarify what you are reading or provide opportunities for practice. Many things that are *not* good for us are habit forming, but effective questioning happens only with practice and it is *very* good for us!

Assessing and recording questions

Since *Asking Better Questions* was first published, we have used the text for our own reference and also as a source for workshops that we were invited to present. Rereading the text, we discovered that much of what we had to say was still relevant and quotations that still apply we have kept. For this edition, we used the latest scholarship as a gloss on the earlier research, enabling readers to consider the history of questioning as strategy and technique and, in particular, the pedagogical rationale for questioning as a means of educating citizens. *Tout ça change; tous c'est le même chose.* Changing the way we educate is like turning the *Queen Mary II* around in the St. Lawrence River—it takes a long time—but that doesn't mean we shouldn't keep on turning!

We all know how to ask questions—after all, we have been doing it almost since we could talk—but as you likely realize, becoming an *effective* questioner is hard. It takes time and it takes diligence. Think how long it took you to learn to type or to know what seasoning would make that recipe taste better. Give yourself time and permission to try things out and keep on working away at it. Let your students in on your quest—they can help you and themselves. One day, you will notice that it is beginning to happen without as much effort. You will realize that you have asked spontaneously a question that really shook up your students and made them think—and made *you* think, too.

Apart from the questions that you will discover through the activity sheets in this resource, you might like to keep a file of questions that proved effective in your lessons, whether you had planned them or they arrived spontaneously as part of the classroom conversation. Remember to record the questions students ask as they are also useful to consider when you are re-planning. Note any questions you come across in your reading that make you think. That is how we found many of the questions you see in the sidebars. It's a useful exercise that somehow doesn't interfere with enjoyment. Remember, wonderful questions may be found in all sorts of writing and when you apprentice yourself to them, they become your models for learning.

Keep Eric Booth's advice in mind as you start your travels through this book.

The key question is not whether schools can support the development of democratic citizens, but whether they choose to make this goal more than a rhetorical priority.
—Joel Westheimer and Joseph Kahne (2003, p. 12)

Posing questions is the central act of reading the world: it must become a habit. I wish I could give you a handy kitbag of reliable questions to try, but there can be no prescribable set of sure-fire questions. The whole game is one giant improvisation . . . the questions themselves are far less important that the habit of questioning.
—Eric Booth (1999, p. 210)

Chapter 1   What Seems to Be the Problem?

Let us . . . make the study of the art of question-asking one of the central disciplines in language education.
—Neil Postman (1979, p. 140)

The value of questions is grossly overlooked in the high-demand, quick-fix nature of our lives and our nation. We are answer-oriented everywhere, having been trained to this through schooling that is almost entirely right-answer driven. Scant notice is ever given to the quality of our questions. The rebellious anger of many young adults is (and perhaps always has been) fuelled by the inattention or weak answering they encounter to their good hard questions. No wonder some make habits out of their bad answers.
—Eric Booth (1999, p. 103)

From his earliest writings, Neil Postman has affirmed that questioning is as much a language art as reading and writing. "In the development of intelligence," he writes in *Teaching as a Conserving Activity*, "nothing can be more 'basic' than learning how to ask productive questions" (1979, p. 140). He has also said he is "astonished" to see how questioning remains neglected.

We, too, are astonished (to borrow Postman's word) that, in the matter of question-making and question-asking, the message about productive questions is still not getting through. There may be texts on questioning (see Bibliography), a great many interesting articles and theses on questioning, and, of course, faculties and colleges of education dealing with questioning as a component of teaching methodology; however, in everything we have read, seen, heard, or experienced, the emphasis seems to be on theory and the theory of practice. Instead, the focus should be on the everyday practicalities of classroom interaction: the "what is happening" engagement of teacher and students with the subject.

Interestingly, the books and articles on questioning published in the last decade have not been about questioning at all; they have been about those concerns that can be explored substantially only when we know how to ask the kinds of questions that will help us understand what is happening and why it is happening and reveal possibilities that may offer solutions. These are written for the public and address such issues as citizenship and democracy, war and peace, and creativity as a requirement for closing the ingenuity gap. The kinds of questions that authors such as Saul and Noddings raise, as well as their concerns about our ability to begin to think of these questions—let alone raise them—are compelling and urgent. Their questions set an agenda for a curriculum that is not so much different in its content as different in how that content is delivered, made use of, and reflected upon.

We work with classroom teachers, teachers who supervise teaching practice in their classrooms, teachers-in-training, and teacher-educators. They all know that whatever the plan, strategy, or technique, effective teaching depends primarily upon the teacher's skill in being able to ask questions that generate different kinds of learning. They are aware that questions must draw on the wide learning possibilities inherent in the subject material; at the same time, they recognize that good, or effective, questions require the sort of vitality that challenges students to approach their learning creatively.

If you are a classroom teacher, you may recognize one or two of these quotes as part of your experience:

"We had a wonderful discussion in class today. I've no idea why it went so well."

"You'd think they'd be interested in the rain forest situation after that super film. But could I get the discussion going? No way! They sat around like they'd been hit on the head!"

"I asked some really 'higher-order questions' to get them thinking. I got nothing but 'low-level' answers!"

"My problem with asking questions is that once they get going they won't shut up. I really don't have that kind of time."

If you are a teacher-in-training, a teaching practice supervisor, or a teacher-educator, you may find a few of these statements familiar.

"Ms. Young will never be an asset to the teaching profession until she gains more experience in questioning."

"John is a lovely person who loves kids and will be a wonderful teacher when he improves his questioning skills."

"I think I was asking some good questions today, but my supervisor is concerned that I was losing control. How do I convince her that I wanted the students to talk among themselves as well as with me?"

"The problem with Mr. Auld is that I get so interested in what he's teaching that I wish I was part of the class. I want to answer his questions instead of analysing them!"

As a student now or in the past, do any of these comments resonate with you?

"Ms. Brown asked only one question today and we kicked it around for the rest of the class—in fact, we're still talking about it!"

"Why should I bother to tell him the answer when he already knows it?"

"She knows I know the answers, so she never asks me anymore."

"The teacher asks us questions to make us look stupid so he can show off what he knows about everything."

Apart from the familiarity and, for some of us, a nostalgic recognition that the more things change, the more they remain the same, what could these comments be telling us? Here are some possible ideas.

- A good question is seductive; like a work of art, the response it generates is for enjoyment, not analysis!
- If you don't know what makes a good question, it is difficult to recognize one.
- Those who understand the value of questions do not necessarily know how to make questions relevant to their students' experience.
- Teachers often do not realize, or cannot accept, that a good question generates a silence filled with thought which leads to talk.
- Teachers are often worried by the consequences of effective questioning because of the noise of vital talk; the perceived lack of control (perceived by whom?—the principal? self? students?); the inability to handle misinformation as it circulates in the talk; the loss of time from

Just when education appeared to be ready to shift into new, more pedagogically effective paradigms, world events interfered, people became fearful and education swung back to a conservative agenda that privileges right-answer testing. It is a little sad to realize that what we wrote in 1991 still applies. The question, of course, is sad for whom?

curriculum coverage, and the difficulty of involving those students who are not overtly participating.

- The significance of peer talk to the learning process is often undervalued.
- Teachers tend to lose their confidence when in the same position as their students: pursuing a question without one right answer.
- With the pressure of high-stakes standardized testing, teachers become uncomfortable using time-consuming strategies that cannot be measured in traditional ways.
- Teachers may not recognize that they are using questions as part of their discipline and control agenda.
- Some people still misunderstand the nature of education. They perceive knowledge as immutable and learning as knowing the right answer.
- Quantity experience is not the same as quality experience: the more questions you ask does not make you a better questioner; it only helps you ask more questions in a shorter time.

In a survey of curriculum documents, the characteristics of a citizen of the 21st century were detailed as follows: flexibility, technological taste, freedom from biases, the development of self-efficacy, satisfaction in leisure, effective and sensitive communication, love of lifelong, rigorous learning, and responsible citizenship.

Given the present environment in teaching, it is understandable that there is a reluctance to break from traditional structures however much we would like to engage in more classroom discourse and however much we are told the value of that discourse to the learning process. We believe, though, that effective education is a major means by which we can help our students prepare for their futures—and that the ability to question is fundamental to envisioning that future.

How do we view the student in the educational process?

We all know that education is concerned with the development of the whole student, who can be seen in terms of three parts:

1. What the student thinks and knows—the Cognitive Domain
2. What the student feels about what he thinks and knows—the Affective Domain
3. What the student does as a result of his knowledge, thoughts, and feelings—the Psychomotor Domain

No part is more or less important than another and the overriding educational goals in all curricula are to show that the whole is greater than the sum of its parts.

If you accept that you cannot separate feeling from thinking and doing, then you may have little difficulty in recognizing a good question and what makes it work. Everything that goes on in the classroom, but most specifically in good questioning, must be presented in such a way that it connects with the students at both an intellectual and a *feeling* level. Teachers may teach as diligently as they can, but learners will not learn unless they *want* to learn. This truth is something that everyone has always known.

So, why is it that schools tend to concentrate on the cognitive and psychomotor development of their students and leave the affective to educate itself? This issue is one of assessment. A fact is a public thing;

knowledge is public. Both facts and knowledge can be shared and objectively measured (for the most part). But emotions, attitudes, values, and beliefs are regarded as personal and, therefore, private. Such things can be assessed only subjectively, if at all. And yet, Antonio Damasio (1999) states that our feelings are what inform reasoning and that without them, our decision-making is devoid of good sense. If he is right, then we surely have to recognize the place (and the power) of feelings in our students' thoughts.

It is not surprising that traditionally private matters have had no place in the educational system. In the nineteenth-century view of society, everything had its place. Matters of the spirit belonged in the church, domestic affairs in the home, business in the workplace, "book-learning" in schools and universities, sex in marriage, and feelings locked in the heart.

Today, the view is very different. With changing societal patterns and the universalization of education, teachers are required to be responsible for the domestic, moral, career, and health education of their students —what the Center for the Study of Teaching and Policy describes as "the flood of non-academic problems that contemporary students bring to school" (1998, p. 3). Despite that significant change, the nineteenth-century view of schools as places where factual knowledge is acquired and the affective domain is ignored persists. (See Egan, 1987.) This attitude is reinforced by high-stakes, standardized testing and the demand for accountability.

Although there have been scholarly studies that refer to the importance of the affective domain, most educational practice still seems to be influenced by the traditional tenet that the student is a sponge to soak up information, a *tabula rasa* to be written upon by the teacher, a jug to be filled with knowledge. Certainly, psychologists in general, as James Britton (1970, p. 217) points out, have "traditionally concentrated upon cognitive organization and tended to regard emotion as itself disorganized and *possessing a disorganizing influence*" (italics ours).

Such a situation is no longer tenable because today we know much more about the effects of the emotions on performance. It has been recognized that a positive feeling can enhance physical and mental prowess; an inviting atmosphere can promote school success; and a sense of self-esteem will develop when students see that they *own* their learning (Purkey, 1978). "'Reluctant' students who are encouraged to become active participants in classroom interaction have a greater chance of becoming responsible and vigorous learners (Hannam, et al., 1977).

What is a vigorous learner?

The traditional view of participation has suggested that students are in the passive mode (or, more accurately, the "done to" mode); that student participation involves taking in who, what, and how, absorbing, being acted upon, and giving back without additions and elaborations. Of course, this type of participation has its place in the teaching–learning interaction and there are times when it is effective; the concern is that it not strangle initiative nor inhibit the contributions of the learner. Garrison warns us that, "the obsession with coverage leads to bored students who are rarely engaged in their own learning" (2003, p. 571).

Happily, "participation" in most classrooms today means that students are in the *active* mode. They are not only taking in, absorbing, and being acted upon, but working energetically, acting upon their initiatives, acting upon others (peers *and* teacher), asking questions, and understanding that they have the right (and the responsibility) to contribute their ideas, experiences, and feelings about the content and procedures of the lesson.

Effective teaching depends upon recognizing that effective *learning* takes place when the students are vigorous participants in what's going on. And for effective teaching and learning to occur, teachers must structure their teaching to invite and sustain that active participation. They need to provide experiences that get students thinking and feeling, get the adrenalin flowing, and generate in students a need for expression.

We do our students a disservice when we ignore the whole person. If we think we can educate only by considering the intellect, we mislead ourselves, and if we see teachers solely as transmitters and students solely as receivers, we limit the power of learning.

We believe that questions from both teachers *and* students have the power to generate vivid ideas, spur the imagination, and provoke both teacher and student into a shared, creative learning experience.

There are, of course, implications in all of this:

- Effective questions generate student thinking and interest in making answers.
- Thoughts take time to formulate.
- Ideas need to be expressed and tested out.
- To be an effective questioner, you may have to develop the patience to wait for answers to be formulated, the skill of listening so that you will know how to respond, and the finesse to "send the ball back" in such a way that your students perceive learning as a dialogue: a dialogue in which everyone's thoughts, feelings, and actions matter.
- As the classroom becomes an exchange for the expression of ideas, you may have to offer different strategies and techniques for covering subject areas. You may also have to rethink your planning and assessment strategies and techniques in order to fit new teaching approaches.
- Your position in the classroom will change as your students come to see you not only as someone with answers, but also as someone who is seeking answers, someone who would rather have a classroom full of unanswered questions than unquestioned answers.

Before you throw up your hands, throw away this book, or think that you will have to abandon all your strategies and techniques—relax! We are not talking new philosophies, new methodologies, or clean slates, but rather a transformation of what you already know and practise into something that, we hope, will be more interesting, challenging, and valuable for you and your students.

We begin by examining the structure of knowing, or cognition, as it has been applied to the theory and practice of questioning. We expect you already know a bit about this, and that is always a good place to start.

Chapter 2   A Question of Thinking

Here's an example of what we mean about the influence of Bloom's taxonomy:

Use an appropriate variety and mix of questions. One good strategy is to start with convergent questions and then continue with divergent questions, perhaps asking questions in hierarchical sequence and building from the recall of facts to higher levels of thinking and problem-solving. If a question requiring a higher level thinking skill stymies the student, go down to a question requiring a lower-level thinking skill and then *work up the hierarchy* [italics ours].
—U. of Alabama School of Medicine, Office of Curriculum Development & Management, 2006

Even now, when we consider the development of thinking skills, we turn for guidance to what is commonly known as Bloom's taxonomy. This hierarchical system can be found in *The Taxonomy of Educational Objectives: The Classification of Educational Goals, Handbook 1, Cognitive Domain* by Benjamin S. Bloom and David R. Krathwohl (1965). To summarize, this taxonomy suggests that you cannot value or judge something until you (a) know the facts, (b) understand the facts, (c) can apply the facts, (d) can take the facts apart, and (e) can put the facts together in such a way that new perspectives are revealed. The significance of the authors' work in clarifying the processes of logical thinking is undeniable and their contribution to education is great.

In new materials on questioning, though, there are indications that it is the *kind* of thinking/feeling that needs to be exercised rather than the order provided by the taxonomy that matters. Despite that, the literature—especially in teacher education—still implies that because they generate thinking, questions should follow the same hierarchical structure from the simple (recall) to the complex (evaluation). We believe that such a practice has resulted in distorting the place of questioning in teaching:

- Simple factual recall questions are often not interesting ways of beginning an inquiry—they are not attention-grabbers—they do, however, save time.
- It is foolish to suppose that asking a simple question generates only simple thinking. The question "Is the sun shining?" could cause your students to think in all sorts of different ways, particularly if the answer is yes and they are wondering if you've gone blind or are merely trying a coy way of introducing a science lesson!
- Questions should spring from interest on the part of the teacher and of the students. A structure that *dictates* the order of procedure can inhibit natural inquiry. The following example demonstrates what we are talking about.

A young teacher in a rural township in Australia is earnestly setting out a series of questions which will explore and develop her primary students' understanding of cities. You will note how carefully she has followed the structure of Bloom's taxonomy. She has invested much time and thought on her lesson plan because she hopes to be able to use it many times during her teaching career!

We are indebted to Carole Tarlington, artistic director of the Vancouver Youth Theatre, for this example of a teacher's lesson plan.

The Taxonomy of Educational Objectives

Lower Order
1. Knowledge
Recalling what we already know
2. Comprehension
Demonstrating what we understand through negotiating what we know into different patterns of information
3. Application
Applying what we have learned to other situations

Higher Order
4. Analysis
Reasoning our ideas into logical patterns of understanding
5. Synthesis
Constructing new ideas from what is known
6. Evaluation
Valuing what is implicit in our thinking

Based on Bloom and Krathwohl, 1965

Her plan is to show a big poster of a busy harbor scene in New York City. These are the questions she will ask:

Question 1 (*Knowledge*)
What do you see in this picture?
Question 2 (*Comprehension*)
What do we call places like that?
Question 3 (*Application*)
Do you know of any other places that look like this picture?
Question 4 (*Analysis*)
Why are there so many policemen in the picture?
Question 5 (*Synthesis*)
What if there were no policemen?
Question 6 (*Evaluation*)
Would you rather live in a city that size or in a small town? Why?

When she asked the first question, a student replied, "It's a picture of New York after a robbery. I wouldn't want to live in that dangerous city."

Well? How would you fill in the next 30 minutes?

Suppose the teacher had started out by asking the following question, which is simply Question 6, her evaluation question, rephrased?

"I wonder how our lives would be different if we lived here?"

Might she not have satisfied her lesson objectives and generated a more satisfying discussion for everyone?

As a structure, the taxonomy is not—nor was it designed to be—a constructive way of planning and asking questions. Bloom and Krathwohl's research is about *knowing* and as such, it helps us see the kinds of thinking we can set into action through questions.

So, what is thinking?

Many words describe the ways we think. For example, consider this list from the New South Wales Education Department:

Connecting	Contrasting	Rehearsing	Inducing
Arguing	Projecting	Testing	Approximating
Convincing	Questioning	Clarifying	Selecting
Generating	Reconciling	Reflecting	Deducing
Analysing	Suspending	Judging	Generalizing
Capitulating	Wondering	Disrupting	Alluding
Relating	Rejecting	Cooperating	Solving
Composing	Hazarding	Synchronizing	Matching
Retracting	Modifying	Harmonizing	Probing
Associating	Including	Speculating	Eliciting
Sequencing	Inventing	Contradicting	Soliciting
Suggesting	Extending	Assimilating	Recalling
Sorting	Accommodating	Empathizing	Calculating
Imagining	Proving	Compromising	Formulating
Comparing	Hypothesizing	Refuting	Valuing
Intuiting	Refining	Internalizing	Reminiscing
Predicting	Improving	Abstracting	

Some words mean almost the same thing (e.g., recalling, remembering, and reminiscing), and others describe quite different ways of thinking. For instance, calculating is not the same as formulating, reasoning is different from imagining, and judging is, when you think about it, not quite the same as evaluating. Just as some people have lived their whole lives using only a limited vocabulary so it is possible to live within a narrow lexicon of thinking skills. If you are in the profession of educating, though, you are required to provide students with more than just enough to get by on.

The more opportunities the teacher gives students to think about the same thing in different ways and different things in the same way, the more agile their minds will become. So, when an effective teacher is planning questions or taking part in dialogue with her students, she considers these two things:

1. What kinds of thinking is this question generating?
2. How will this question help my students engage in and with the material?

"Where is the boy . . . ?": Kinds of thinking

To illustrate, we have chosen to use a simple source with questions formulated according to Bloom and Krathwohl's categories. The questions are geared to two different age groups—primary and secondary—and you will notice that the same question can often be asked of both groups. We have selected some answers to illustrate the variety of thinking that one question can generate. And because we now know that thinking cannot be disassociated from feeling, at the end of each section we ask a question designed to help you reflect on how students' thoughts and feelings might be engaging with the material.

> Little Boy Blue, come blow your horn,
> The cow's in the meadow, the sheep's in the com,
> Where is the boy who looks after the sheep?
> He's under the haystack, fast asleep.

Students also saw an illustration accompanying the nursery rhyme, only one of a number of sources used in teaching these units.

- Teaching unit for primary students:
  Environmental Studies—Children Everywhere
- Teaching unit for secondary students:
  Social History—A Study of Children in Victorian Times
- Teaching objective:
  To see our own situation more clearly as a result of studying our past

1. Questions that draw upon knowledge (Remembering)

Do we want our students to tell us what they already know through what we have taught them, what others (teachers, friends, parents, etc.)

have taught them, what they have perceived and experienced for themselves? If the answer is yes, some of the thinking skills are as follows:

recalling   remembering   recognizing   recollecting   defining   identifying

This type of question is often characterized by key words such as these:

Remembering
Who . . . ?
What . . . ?
Where . . . ?
When . . . ?
How . . . ?

Who? What? Where? When? How?

Question (Primary):
In this picture, what is the color of the boy's coat?
Answers:
Blue.
Sort of blue.
Bluey-green.

Question (Secondary):
Where would you find a haystack today?
Answers:
In the fields.
In barns.
I don't think we still have them.

What in these teacher-posed questions might make you want to answer them?

---

2. Questions that test comprehension (Understanding)

Do we want our students to demonstrate that they understand what they know through negotiating what is known into different patterns of information? If the answer is yes, these are some of the thinking skills:

rewording   rephrasing   comparing   explaining   interpreting   describing   illustrating   associating   differentiating

This type of question is often characterized by phrases such as these:

Understanding
What is meant by . . . ?
Can you rephrase . . . ?
Can you describe . . . ?
What's the difference . . . ?
What is the main idea?

What is meant by? Can you rephrase? Can you describe? What is the difference? What is the main idea?

Question (Primary):
Can you describe his coat in your own words?
Answers:
His coat is the color of the sky.
It looks just like Mary's coat.
It is a funny sort of jackety-thing.

Question (Secondary):
What is the difference between the appearance of the shepherd in the picture and a shepherd today?
Answers:
I don't think there is much difference.
Do shepherds carry crooks today?

Shepherds today are usually grown men . . . and women, too.

> What intrigues you about these teacher-posed questions?

3. Questions that require application (Solving)

Do we want our students to be able to select, transfer, and use information and generalizations to complete a task through taking what they have already learned and applying it to other situations? If the answer is yes, some of the thinking skills are these:

problem-solving exampling classifying selecting transferring applying hypothesizing relating

This type of question is often characterized by phrases such as these:

Solving
Whom would you choose?
What might happen if . . . ?
How can . . . ?
What examples . . . ?
How would you . . . ?

Whom would you choose? What might happen if . . . ? How can . . . ?
What examples . . . ? How would you . . . ?

Question (Primary and Secondary):
Who do you know who reminds you of Little Boy Blue?
Answers (Primary):
Mary has a coat the same color.
My brother, he sleeps a lot!
My friend lives on a sheep farm.
Answers (Secondary):
I saw something on TV about child labor in Third World countries.
Remember the security guy who fell asleep and the bank was robbed?
My cousin walks dogs when their owners are away.

> What might account for these responses being different from those of the previous categories?

4. Questions that encourage analysis (Reasoning)

Do we want our students to be able to support their arguments and opinions through organizing ideas into logical patterns of understanding? If the answer is yes, some of the thinking skills are as follows:

analysing determining the evidence drawing conclusions reasoning logically reasoning critically inferring ordering

This type of question is often characterized by words or phrases such as these:

Reasoning
I wonder why . . . ?
I wonder what would happen . . . ?
What if . . . ?
What could have been the . . . ?
Is it a fact that . . . ?
Should we assume that . . . ?

I wonder why . . . ? I wonder what would happen . . . ? What if . . . ?
What could have been the . . . ? Is it a fact that . . . ? Should we assume that . . . ?

Question (Primary and Secondary):
Why might he have fallen asleep?
Answers (Primary):
He was sick.
He was lazy.
He'd stayed up too late watching TV.
Answers (Secondary):
He probably had another job at night.
Kids in those days weren't very well fed and they slept, sometimes, six to a bed.
He was counting his sheep and just fell asleep!

What is there about this question that prompts such a variety of answers?

---

5. Questions that invite synthesis (Creating)

Do we want our students to construct a connected whole from separate elements through expressing original and creative ideas? If the answer is yes, some of the thinking skills are as follows:

originating integrating combining predicting designing developing improving reflecting supposing

Creating
How could we/you . . . ?
How can . . . ?
What if . . . ?
I wonder how . . . ?
Do you suppose that . . . ?

This type of question is often characterized by phrases such as these:

How could we/you . . . ? How can . . . ? What if . . . ?
I wonder how . . . ? Do you suppose that . . . ?

Question (Primary):
I wonder how he will explain to the farmer how the cow got into the corn?
Answers:
I think he should tell the farmer the truth.
I'd say someone left the gate open . . . after all, they could have.
He was away looking for a little lamb that was lost.

Question (Secondary):
I wonder how it is possible to solve the problem of students holding jobs while they are still in school?
Answers:
I wonder what would happen if they passed a Student Labor Law so that no one under eighteen could hold a job?
Maybe we could go to school for a semester, then take off a semester to earn money. I wouldn't mind that!
I don't see this as a problem. Most kids do it and we need the money!

What kinds of feelings generated by these teacher-posed questions might lead to these answers?

---

6. Questions that promote evaluation (Judging)

Do we want our students to consider the values implicit in their thinking through looking at evidence and establishing criteria? If the answer is yes, some of the thinking skills are as follows:

summarizing judging defending assessing arguing reasoning appraising criticizing appreciating selecting deducing deciding priorities

Judging
Which might be better . . . ?
Does it matter . . . ?
Would you agree that . . . ?
Would it be better if . . . ?
What is your opinion . . . ?
I wonder if we (you/they) were right to . . . ?

This type of question is often characterized by phrases such as these:

Which might be better? Does it matter . . . ? Would you agree that . . . ? Would it be better if . . . ? What is your opinion . . . ? I wonder if we (you/they) were right to . . . ?

Question (Primary):
Does it matter if he falls asleep if no one ever finds out?
Answers:
I don't think he'd feel good about it.
I don't think it matters . . . well, maybe it might.
He'd get found out anyway, 'cause the cow's in the corn!

Question (Secondary):
Would it not be better if the government took over all the financial responsibility for parenting?
Answers:
They'd certainly expect some sort of return for their money.
I think, maybe, there are some countries that do that sort of thing.
It would have to begin with the licensing of couples who want to become parents.

> How does asking students to make judgments give them a sense of control over their learning?

Reflecting on Bloom and Little Boy Blue

Some of the answers here demonstrate different kinds of responses from those the teacher had in mind. For example, the first answer to the primary synthesizing question (see previous page) would appear to be an answer at the evaluation level.

Does it matter? Of course not; you can't *control* thinking; your job is to *generate* thinking.

You will note that some answers are in the form of questions, something that suggests a comfortable classroom. There, students are prepared to ask for facts when they need them, if they aren't sure of them, or if something in their own experience raises a question in their minds, for example: "I wonder what would happen if they passed a Student Labor Law so that no one under eighteen could hold a job?" If teachers confine themselves to questioning from the so-called simple (knowledge) to the complex (evaluation), they may waste a lot of time. In a classroom where students are expected to contribute, most students will ask if they don't know something.

Can you imagine being in a class where the teacher initiates the above lesson by asking,

"What is a haystack? What is a meadow? What is a horn?"

Answer: ZZZZzzzzz.

If you like feeling in command of your class because either you ask questions to which you know the answers or the answers your students give you are unlikely to interfere with what you know, you will tend to question within the first three of Bloom's categories, those described as "lower-order."

Does that mean that a creative teacher should never use questions that fall into those first three categories?

No, of course not. They're important when they *need* to be asked, but do not think you *have* to follow a particular schema when it fails to take into account your students' background, experience, and engagement with the material—these are confederates in learning.

Many of us have problems with the last three or higher-order categories—analysing, synthesizing and evaluating—for any number of reasons. Do any of these apply to you?

- The questions present opportunities for expressing many divergent views.
- The questions offer opportunities for the class, or one or two students, to take over.
- The class may split into factions and argue among themselves.
- The teacher may lose the focus.
- It can be hard to know whether students are being smart-alecks or if they are working at a serious level of thinking. (He was counting his sheep and just fell asleep.)
- Students may introduce things about which the teacher knows little or nothing.
- Discussion may move to a topic or aspect of a topic with which the teacher is uncomfortable.
- Some students will be left behind or left out.
- Sometimes, the discussion will be unproductive, repetitive, or overtaken by personal monologues which are irrelevant.
- It may be difficult to wrap up, bring to a conclusion, or even just stop discussion.
- The teacher may be intimidated by the fact that these last three categories are often referred to as higher-order.

Is this really as bad as it sounds? No, of course not! Like chairing a meeting or running a discussion, you have to keep in mind your focus and know *why* you asked the question(s). If, as a classroom teacher, you can visualize these apparent problems in a positive light, what do you see and hear? You see and hear students actively engaged in their learning, their minds ticking away because you have aroused their interest and they are so involved that they are taking responsibility for maintaining their engagement.

We bring an immense store of beliefs, assumptions, and commonsense knowledge about the world to any statement we hear or read, and we are also influenced by many other factors, including the context of that statement and the speaker's or writer's intentions.
—Thomas Homer-Dixon (2001, p. 269)

Just sit back and keep your eye on which way the wind is blowing, the tides are running and what time you are due in port. Above all, try not to dip your oar into the water too often!

We cannot separate knowledge from feeling. Students and teachers bring their experiences and feelings into the classroom and those are vital components in the process of thinking. James Britton understood the importance of feelings to our thought processes long before Damasio (1994) gave us the proof. "The real danger it seems to me," he wrote, "lies in imposing a disjunction between thought and feeling, between cognitive and affective modes of representation. . . . We need to recognize the value and importance both of discursive, logical organization and at the same time, that of undissociated intuitive processes . . . " (1970, p. 217).

In the next chapter we look at a structure that focuses on the place of feelings in teaching and learning. As the taxonomy of knowing is a guide for generating thinking, so the taxonomy of feeling is a guide for generating students' engagement with the material to be studied. In the words of the old song, "you can't have one without the other."

Chapter 3   A Question of Feeling

Learning has to be felt for it to be effective . . . It is this essential feeling level that is often either not recognized or ignored by teachers. Only when work is at an experiential feeling level can a change of understanding take place.
—Gavin Bolton (1979, p. 31)

. . . effective pedagogy is enhanced by context in which there is an engagement between thinking and feeling, at personal, interpersonal and intrapersonal levels.
—Roslyn Arnold (1998, p. 115)

In the negotiation between teacher, subject, and learner, students often read the teacher's emotional engagement with them and the material more effectively than the teacher is aware of the students' emotional engagement with her and the material. Students may not understand what the teacher is talking about, but they are always aware of the emotional sub-text. It has not occurred to them to separate thought from feeling and yet, as pointed out in Chapters 1 and 2, education has been attempting to do that for a long time.

Learning springs from curiosity, from the *need* to know. A good teacher capitalizes on that innate feeling by attracting, maintaining, and satisfying the attention of learners while giving them something worthwhile to think about. It is the learners who actively go about learning. This appetite is very much like the appetite for food. The first question comes from the one who is hungry, "What's for dinner?" The job of the cook is to provide a meal which is attractive and nutritious and then to stand by offering more when it is needed, suggesting items that might have been overlooked and providing an ambience which encourages digestion. But it is not the cook who picks up the knife and fork and eats. The active engagement of learners with their "food for thought" is what concerns us here.

Professional teacher training concentrates on the cognitive and the physical because they are both capable of measurement and observation. The study of feeling, as the *Encyclopaedia Britannica* (1962, p. 144) points out, is "complicated by the fact that the event being perceived is *not open for direct inspection* by others." Despite this apparent difficulty, teachers—if the quotations in the margin have validity—must pay attention to the fact that their students have lives of feeling. Effective teaching and learning can occur *only* when teachers recognize that thought is unavoidably harnessed to feeling and when they know how to read the signs of that feeling engagement.

The Taxonomy of Personal Engagement

Anyone who is a teacher or who has been a student knows that there are different levels of involvement in any learning experience. We have identified these degrees of involvement:

interest: being curious about what is presented;

engaging: wanting to be, and being involved in the task;

committing: developing a sense of responsibility towards the task;

internalizing: merging objective concepts (the task or what is to be learned) with subjective experience (what is already owned) resulting in understanding and therefore ownership, of new ideas;

interpreting: wanting and needing to communicate that understanding to others;

evaluating: wanting and being willing to put that understanding to the test.

These levels of involvement we call a Taxonomy of Personal Engagement (Morgan and Saxton, 1987, pp. 21–30).

It is possible to recognize the signs of feeling engagement, which point to degrees of involvement. What is gathered from a reading of those signs can inform the teacher so that she can adjust her teaching to the state of her students' engagement. In 2004, the National Survey of Student Engagement (an initiative of the United States) was introduced to Canadian universities. If you were to check out the Internet site, the survey would appear to be exclusively about universities and community colleges; however, it is easily applicable to any educational institution and a useful general guide for those interested in examining how effectively a school is engaging its students. What we are describing below is local and particular to every classroom.

Interest

You will recognize that there are different levels of student involvement in what you are teaching. Some of your students will not be interested, perhaps because what you are offering seems irrelevant or because some private agenda inhibits them from becoming interested. Their lack of interest may be of two types:

- aggressive—yawning, talking to a neighbor, reading a book; and
- passive—more difficult to detect because students often take on the shape of interest but there is "nothing behind the eyes."

Some students will be interested because they like the topic, enjoy you as a teacher, even though the topic doesn't interest them, are curious and want to learn, or like you and are prepared to give you a chance.

Student interest may be evidenced by their willingness to

- make and maintain eye contact; and
- make verbal and non-verbal responses in a supportive, congruent, and appropriate manner.

In other words, students are watching, listening, and responding.

Engaging

Then there are those students who are interested enough to do whatever you want them to do: perform a task, contribute to a discussion, listen actively, and so on. Their engagement is evidenced by their willingness to

- participate;
- follow instructions;
- follow the rules of the classroom; and
- work independently of the teacher, either by themselves or with others.

Students who are engaging with the work generate a positive atmosphere of achieving. This is what principals and head teachers are always hoping to see when they show visitors around the school.

Committing

Other students are really "in gear." They are prepared to accept responsibility for their work by finding and maintaining a focus for themselves and by generating their own ideas, attitudes, and points of view about the material. Their commitment is reflected in these ways:

- absorption in the work (they are often reluctant to move on to new work within the lesson or to abandon it when the bell rings to end the lesson);
- ability to control and manipulate the material for themselves;
- confidence to challenge the direction of the work; and
- the emergence of creative ideas.

Students who are committing demonstrate a high degree of personal investment in the work, something that makes it possible for the next level to come into play.

Internalizing

Nothing is easier to recognize or more difficult to describe in behavioral terms than what happens to those students for whom "the lights are going on." This level of engagement, described by Bruner (1986), Vygotsky (1986), and others as *internalization*, is crucial to long-term understanding. If it is not reached the student will be engaged only in short-term learning and what appears to be understanding will melt away when the need for it disappears. For example, knowledge crammed for a test or examination is forgotten before the holidays have scarcely begun.

In internalizing, the drive to understand is fuelled by feelings of excitement, concentration, perplexity and, often, anxiety. It is followed by feelings of relief, satisfaction, and calm: the mind has moved from confusion to order, from a state of unrelated pieces to a connected whole. The experience is rather like finding the piece of a jigsaw that suddenly reveals a section of the puzzle. You may see this in students as their facial expressions change from concentration to relief or their posture changes from tension to relaxation. Sometimes, the merging appears to be instantaneous: a revelation, the light bulb going on, or, as one student described it, "a sort of gut-thunk!" On the other hand, it may be that you can "see the wheels slowly turning" until that flash of understanding—"Just a moment, everyone. I think I've got it! . . . (pause) . . . Right! Now, I know it!" Here it appears that the student feels he knows, but has to wait for a little while for the intellect to catch up.

Other students intuitively recognize that what they are learning has meaning for them, but it often takes much longer for the personal, empathetic relationship with the new knowledge to develop. It is not until they try to express that meaning (see Interpreting) and to test it out (see Evaluating) that they realize that they do know what they now know.

The result of making these connections is a new realization, a different way of understanding. It is this which establishes for learners a sense of control over what they are learning. Both teacher and students "will have no difficulty in knowing that a shift in understanding has taken place. Call it a 'moment of truth,' an 'aesthetic experience' or 'peak experiencing'" as Maslow (1968, p. 79) does, we do not need a "check list of behavioural evidence to verify that internalization has occurred" (Morgan and Saxton, 1987, p. 25).

Interpreting

Once students have begun to make connections between their own experience and the material they are studying, they can and need to move into another level of engagement. You will recognize those students as the ones who are willing to talk about the work:

- They are anxious to hear what others think and feel and are prepared to defend their points of view and to share their own feelings and opinions.
- They are willing to reconsider their responses and adapt their conclusions in the light of new information and ideas.
- They have the confidence to submit their feelings and ideas for analysis and consideration by others.
- They are anxious to make predictions and to consider the implications of their thinking.
- They are gripped by the possibilities of their new understanding and are eager to make it concrete in some way, perhaps by writing, graphics, debate or applying their conclusions to other situations.

It is worth noting that some students who have undergone a deep internalizing experience will not want to share their thoughts and feelings right away, and sometimes not for a long time. A sensitive teacher will respect this need for privacy and distance.

When education is understood as the construction of meaning, rather than merely the transmission of knowledge, the primacy of the student's engagement in the process becomes self-evident.
—William Garrison (2003, p. 526)

Without language, what concept have we of past or future as separated from the immediate present? Without language, how can we tell anyone what we feel or what we think? . . . without language, how could [we] reach deep inside [ourselves] and discover the truths that are hidden there or find out what emotions [we] share?
—Robertson Davies (1998, pp. 70, 71)

Evaluating

According to the National Survey of Student Engagement (2004), one of the indicators of active and collaborative learning is the willingness to discuss your reading or classes outside of class with other students, family members, or co-workers.

The final level of engagement is revealed when students want to test their new understanding on someone who has not been involved in the process. Students confirm it by trying it out in a more public forum:

- by talking at home about what they understand (often misconstrued by parents as "being preached at!");
- by discussing it with their peers in school but outside the classroom;
- by introducing the ideas in another class; or
- by writing an article for the school paper, and so on.

Ownership through deepening engagement

Placing students' efforts to understand at the centre [means that] the relationship between student and teacher becomes one that is more interactive, complex and unpredictable. This is nothing less than a "re-culturing of the classroom" but one that is important to a "democratically-oriented vision of schools."
—Mark Windschitl (2002, pp. 143, 164)

As indicated earlier, a *taxonomy* is a way of classifying and is cumulative in nature: the next level always builds upon the one before. Because what is happening in a lesson depends on the manner in which you offer the material and also on your students' past experiences and knowledge, students will not likely engage at the same level at the same time; they may also shift back and forth through the levels during the lesson. Students must always move through the sequence, though, if they are to capture the full significance of the work for *them*. Sequential progression is necessary to the deepening of their engagement with, and their eventual ownership of, the material. This "process of ownership," as Malczewski (1990) and Woods (1987) describe it, encourages students to find fresh perspectives and to gain understanding about the issues and materials being explored. This sense of owning, of being in control of their learning, gives students a feeling of increasing satisfaction as they see that what began as the teacher's is becoming their own; as they move from "seeing themselves as people to whom things happen to seeing themselves as people who can make things happen" (Schaffner, 1983, p. 40). Effective teaching requires more than knowing what you are going to teach, why you are teaching it, and to whom you are teaching it. It means recognizing that all students bring their feelings, as well as their minds and bodies, into the classroom. Understanding how you can engage and capitalize on this internal state of needs, preferences, anxieties, curiosity, and excitement will be the dynamic that transforms the classroom into a place where learning is recognized by the students as something to be valued for itself rather than as a means to someone else's evaluation.

True ownership occurs when we see ourselves in the thing owned and recognize that it is an integral part of us.
—Juliana Saxton and Patrick Verriour (1988, pp. 9–10)

The role of the taxonomy in questioning

Here is an exercise: the class is beginning the study of earthworms as part of a unit in Environmental Studies. If you were a student knowing little or nothing about earthworms, which questions would have the greatest potential to engage your interest?

1 How is the earthworm valuable to man?

2 Charles Darwin brought our attention to the value of the earth-worm as a preserver of our heritage. I wonder what he meant?
3 What do you use at the end of your hook when you go fishing?
4 Which would you rather take for a headache: an aspirin or an earthworm?

Why did you choose that particular question?

If you chose 1, it might be because you thought you knew the answer. On the other hand, you might not choose it because you think it's a stupid question—isn't that what you suspect the unit will be about?

If you chose 2, it might be that you wanted to find out the relationship between the lowly earthworm and the Parthenon—a genuine curiosity. On the other hand, you might not choose it because you don't think Charles Darwin sounds very interesting.

If you chose 3, it might be because you learned how to worm a hook this summer and want to share your accomplishment. On the other hand, you might not choose it because you know the answer (doesn't everyone?) and you can't see where the question is going.

If you chose 4, it might be because you had a visceral reaction and are attracted by the macabre. On the other hand, you might not choose it because this book, so far, has given you a headache and the last thing you want to do is to take two worms with a glass of water!

Questions attract students for an infinite number of reasons.

Questions interest them because there is something in them that connects with what is being presented or offered. John Holt (1982, p. 163) writes that learning happens when it becomes important to ask, "What's that, what's it for, how do you work it?" Or to put it another way, learning happens when we are provoked to question. Unless the question holds the possibility of an answer with personal meaning for the student, there can be no change in understanding. The more you know about students' backgrounds, interests, and experiences, the greater chance you have of choosing a question that holds that possibility.

Let's take another example.

You and your English Literature students have just seen a production of Arthur Miller's *The Crucible.* Which of the following questions would have the greatest potential for engaging their interest in discussion?

1 How did the production reflect the atmosphere of the period?
2 What part of the play did you like best? Why?
3 There are many television shows and movies about demonic possession. How do they compare with *The Crucible*?
4 From watching the play, what new insights do you have into the failure of the marriage between John and Elizabeth?

Now, look at all four questions and decide why your students might, or might not, be caught by a particular question. To do this, you do not need to know the play, only to see clearly what each question offers in terms of what you know about the students you teach.

How to use the taxonomy to help frame questions

When we use the taxonomy as a guide for inviting and sustaining students' engagement with the material, we ask ourselves the following:

- What questions shall I ask to attract their attention? *[Interest]*
- What questions shall I ask to draw them into active involvement, where their ideas become an important part of the process? *[Engaging]*
- What questions shall I ask to invite them to take on responsibility for the inquiry? *[Committing]*
- What questions shall I ask to create an environment in which they can reflect upon their thoughts, feelings, attitudes, points of view, experiences, and values in relation to the material? *[Internalizing]*
- What questions shall I ask to invite them to express their understanding of the relationship between their subjective world, the world of their peers, and the world of the subject matter? What opportunities shall I provide to enable them to formulate new questions which arise from their new understanding? *[Interpreting]*
- What questions shall I ask to provide them with opportunities to test their new thinking in different media? *[Evaluating]*

We can see from the Taxonomy of Personal Engagement that a successful lesson depends upon a teacher's awareness of the levels of student engagement and her responses to what she hears and senses as she observes the students working with their peers, the material, and herself. The taxonomy functions in these ways:

- It is the means by which a teacher generates and maintains student involvement in learning.
- It is the agent through which the objective world of the material is brought into a relationship and made congruent with the subjective world of the student, allowing for the possibilities of meaning making.
- It is the process through which students come to control and own their learning.

What are the implications for the teacher?

You will have to learn to see the feeling climate of the classroom as an important indication of the quality of the learning. You must understand that implicit within the Taxonomy of Personal Engagement is the notion of transfer, or *hand over*. Edwards and Mercer (1987, p. 23) call this "the action which signifies the end of the need for a teacher or tutor . . . students come to take control of the process for themselves."

You will find that working with the feeling climate of the classroom will remove you from an adversarial position and put you in a partnership with your students. As they begin to control how they are learning, you, in turn, can spend less time in the roles of disciplinarian and classroom manager. You will be free to take on other teaching stances that can offer you, as well as your students, rich opportunities for learning.

Let us now look at a lesson . . .

. . . when [teaching] is sensitive, intelligent, and creative—those qualities that confer upon it the status of an art—it should, in my view, not be regarded, as it is so often by some, as an expression of unfathomable talent or luck but as an example of humans exercising the highest levels of intelligence. —Elliot Eisner (1994, p. 156)

Chapter 4   The Example Lesson: Snow White

This lesson unit was adapted from the teaching plan, notes, and assessment of a Grade 4 class by Linda Laidlaw, Toronto, November 1988.

We have chosen this lesson because the material with which the teacher is working should be familiar to you, freeing you from a concern with the content, to examine the educational context. We point out the two taxonomies and you will see how Bloom's taxonomy operates non-sequentially. We also point out some of the ways in which the teacher gives her students opportunities to invest themselves in the material and to control the course of the exploration.

Class Description
Subject: Language Arts/Art
Class: Grade 4 (10 years old)
Type: 30 students—16 boys, 14 girls (mixed ethnic backgrounds)
General Characteristics: The class shows a poor command of English. Members are reluctant to speak and to read. Their behavior is restless —they are just able to sit still and listen. The students have low self-esteem.
Teacher's Objectives: To provide the kind of opportunity that will encourage students to listen, to use language, to succeed, to express their feelings through other media (writing and art)

The lesson plan

Consider some reasons for offering these lessons in the afternoons rather than the mornings.

Number of lessons: 2 or 3

Time: 1 hour (afternoons)

1. Explain what the class is going to do:
   • Show picture of castle?

PQ1: What kinds of people might live in a building like this?

Knowing	Engagement	Controlling/ Owning
(1) Applying	Interest	Students' input

- Connect to soap operas on TV?

PQ2: Stories of long ago had the same kind of violence and magic as you see on TV. Can we all go back to those dark and dangerous times?

Knowing	Engagement	Controlling/ Owning
(2) Recalling	Engaging	Students' agreement

2. Let them give suggestions for the names of a girl and a boy.
3. Tell them I will be taking a role in the story and so will they. (Demonstrate?)
4. Tell story of Snow White up to Huntsman's dilemma, then go into role as the Huntsman. Students may need some reminding of story. Hope not.

PQ3: Do you think I should obey the order of the Queen and kill the Princess? (Acknowledge the difficulty of the problem, but keep the story going—focus on the drama.)

Knowing	Engagement	Controlling/ Owning
(3) Judging	Engaging	Opportunity for control

5. Read the next bit till Queen goes to the Apothecary.

PQ4: Can you sell me some poison? How much will you sell me? (If they won't give, go back to story and say the Queen will make her own out of deadly nightshade!)

Knowing	Engagement	Controlling/ Owning
(4) Judging	Engaging	Opportunity for control

6. Tell story to the point where Queen wants to put poison in the apples.

PQ5: How would someone poison an apple?
(Try for pair work here.)

Knowing	Engagement	Controlling/ Owning
(5) Recalling/ Creating	Committing	Opportunity for control

7. Continue story to the selling of the apples.

PQ6: Will you buy one of my lovely, red apples?
(Offer to at least six students.)

What the Teacher Is Promoting		
Knowing	Engagement	Controlling/Owning
(6) Applying/ Judging/ Recalling	Committing	Opportunity for control

8. Shift gears—try to surprise students by moving in a different direction.

PQ7: How do I get to the miners' house?

Knowing	Engagement	Controlling/Owning
(7) Creating/ Judging	Committing	Opportunity for control

9. On with the story to the end of the visit with Snow White. Get them to tell the story of the witch and the apples—to me? to a partner?

PQ8: What happened in the village today?

Knowing	Engagement	Controlling/Owning
(8) Creating	Engaging	Opportunity for ownership

10. On to introduce the Prince (name they gave me).
Task: Draw and/or write the end of the story.

PQ9: A lot of stories end happily ever after. What is the end of your story?

Knowing	Engagement	Controlling/Owning
(9) Creating/ Recalling/ Reasoning	Committing/ Interpreting	Opportunity for ownership

11. Put pictures on wall (Parents' Night date?) and read the end of the story.

Administration: Check supplies, crayons, paint, water tins, paper, copy of *Life* magazine with castles in it. Music? Parents' Night date?

The lesson: What actually happened

Session 1

Teacher: When we were in the library yesterday, many of you chose stories about magic and witches. Today, I'm going to tell you a story about those things but I'm going to need your help.

Q1: How did Mr. Longstaffe [a visiting storyteller] start his story yesterday?

Where something like Q1 appears, it refers to questions that the teacher asked her class; similarly, where something like R1 appears, it refers to student responses.

What the Teacher Is Promoting		
Knowing	Engagement	Controlling/ Owning
(1) Recalling	Interest	Students' input

R1: He said, "This happened a long time ago." (*Two other similar replies*)
Teacher: Good. That's the kind of help I am going to need today.

Q2: Before I begin, can you give me names for a girl and a boy that are different from all the names in our class? They will be the names of the heroine and the hero, so you will need to think about this and choose carefully.

(2) Recalling/ Understanding	Engaging	Opportunity for ownership

R2: *After a number of suggestions, the students choose the names Linda and Emilio, and are thanked.*

Teacher Narration:

Once upon a time, there was a little girl who lived with her father. Her mother had died when she was ten. Her father was a King and so she was a Princess. One day her father came to her and told her that he wished to marry again. When the little girl, whose name was Linda, met her stepmother-to-be, she saw she was a very beautiful woman, who seemed kind and interested in her. She was not surprised that her father, the King, was in love with the woman.

In her narration, the teacher supports the students' contributions in order to promote ownership.

As time went on, Linda began to understand that the most important thing in her stepmother's life was neither Linda nor Linda's father, but her own beauty. The Queen, for that was what she now was, went every day to her magic mirror . . .

R3: *A student says, "I know that story." Teacher acknowledges with a conspiratorial smile.*

. . . and asked it to tell her who was the most beautiful woman in the kingdom. And every day the mirror replied that it was the Queen herself.

Now one day, when the Queen went to her mirror and asked it the question she asked every day, the mirror replied,

"Though you, O Queen, are very fair,
Linda is she beyond compare."

And the Queen fell into a rage and called to her Huntsman and ordered him to take Linda into the depths of the forest and kill her. The Huntsman was appalled that he should be ordered to kill Linda, and all day and all night he wrestled with his conscience. In despair, he went to his closest friend whom he loved and trusted, and said to him . . .

Q3 Teacher (as the Huntsman): I don't know what to do. I've known Linda all her life. What do you think I should do?

What the Teacher Is Promoting

Knowing	Engagement	Controlling/Owning

(3) Solving	Engaging	Opportunity for control

R4: *Teacher turns to a student who looks at her wide-eyed.*
Q4: Do you think I should obey the order of the Queen and kill Linda?

(4) Judging	Engaging	Opportunity for control

R5: I don't know.
Q5: It is difficult, isn't it?

(5) Judging	Engaging	_____

She turns to three other students, repeating Question 4, adding, "What should I do?"

(4a) Judging	Engaging	Opportunity for control

R6: You should kill her.
Teacher as the Huntsman: Then I would be obeying the Queen's orders.
R7: I don't think you should.
Teacher (as the Huntsman): Some of my friends are telling me "yes" and some are telling me "no." I will use their advice to make up my own mind.

Teacher Narration:
The Huntsman thought long and hard, but in the end he could not kill Linda. He took her into the dark forest and told her what the Queen had wanted him to do; then, leaving her with a little food, he ran away himself from the Queen's vengeance.

When the Queen went to her mirror the next day, she was expecting a very different answer from the one she received:
"Though you, O Queen, are very fair, Linda is she beyond compare." And the Queen fell into a rage. She knew that the Huntsman had failed her and now she must do the wicked deed herself. She went to the Apothecary, the one who makes medicines, and said to him . . .

Q6 Teacher (as the Queen): Do you know who I am? *She approaches a student.*

(6) Recalling	Interest	_____

What the Teacher Is Promoting

Knowing	Engagement	Controlling/Owning

R8: No.

Q7 Teacher (as the Queen): I am the Queen. Do you know why I am here?

(7) Recalling	Interest	_____

R9: No.

Q8: I am here to buy poison. Will you sell me some?

(8) Understanding/ Judging	Engaging	_____

R10: No.

Teacher (as the Queen): Thank you. I will now go and ask the apothecary down the road. *She tries another student.*

Q9: Do you know who I am?

(9) Recalling	Interest>Engaging	_____

R11: You're the Queen.

Q10: Do you know why I am here?

(10) Recalling	Interest>Engaging	_____

R12: You want to buy some poison.

Q11 Teacher (as the Queen): Will you sell me some?

(11) Understanding/ Judging	Engaging	Opportunity for control

R13: How much do you want? *He gives her some.*

Teacher (as the Queen): Thank you. *She moves to the next student who tells her before she says anything . . .*

R14: My mother keeps rat poison in the cupboard. I'm not allowed there.

Teacher (as the Queen): That poison must be very strong. I'm sorry you can't give me any. *She turns to the next student.*

Q12 Teacher (as the Queen): Do you have any poison that will kill very big rats?

| What the Teacher Is Promoting | | |
Knowing	Engagement	Controlling/ Owning
(12) Recalling/ Understanding/ Reasoning	Engaging> Committing	Opportunity for control

R15: How much do you need?
Q13 Teacher (as the Queen): How much do you think I should have?

(13) Recalling/ Judging	Committing	Opportunity for control

R16: This much. *Student hands her something.*
The teacher in role turns to three more students and asks them Q12 and Q13.
R17: *All three students give her some poison.*

Teacher Narration:
When the Queen felt that she had enough poison, she went down the stone steps where the apples are stored. She filled two baskets to the top with beautiful, red apples—the best that she could find. She poured all the poisons she had collected into her large black kettle and, while it was cooking, she sat down to think how she would put the poison into the apples so that no one would know.
The teacher confirms contributions, providing opportunities for ownership.

Q14 Teacher (out of role): How would she have done that?

(14) Solving	Engaging	Opportunity for control

R18: *No reply.*
Q15: How could someone poison an apple so that no one would know the poison was there? Just talk to the person next to you.

(15) Recalling/ Solving	Interest>Engaging	Opportunity for control

R19: *Most students have difficulty in working with a partner, not because they aren't interested but because they have difficulty in listening to the other's suggestions. The teacher collects their ideas. These include using a needle, dipping the apple into the poison, using a laser, making an apple pie, and making a spell.*

Teacher Narration:
Soon she had a basketful of poisoned apples which looked just like the basket of good apples. No one could tell the difference. The Queen sent out her spies all over the land and it soon became clear to her that there was only one place that Linda could be. In the depths of the dark forest,

in a glade, there was a little cabin in which the King's gold miners lived. It was rumored that they were harboring a young woman who was working as their housekeeper. Although no one had ever seen her, rumor had it that she was gentle, kind, and loving. Some said that they had heard she was the King's daughter, whom no one had seen for many months.

And so the Queen disguised herself as an itinerant merchant—a purveyor of small goods: needles, threads and other useful household items—and she took upon herself the clothing and appearance of an old woman. She picked up both baskets of apples and walked to the village at the edge of the wood. She came to the first house and knocked on the door.

The teacher takes back control to keep the story on track.

Q16 Teacher (as the Queen): Would you like, sir, to buy one of my beautiful, red, rosy apples?

| (16) Judging | Engaging> Committing | Opportunity for control |

R20: No, thank you. *The teacher turns to another student, who without being asked, says,*

R21: No, thank you. We don't like apples. *She turns to another student who, again without being asked, says,*

R22: (*pointing to the "good" apples*) I'll have an apple from that basket. *The teacher continues the business, with most children accepting an apple from the "good" basket. She turns to the group.*

Q17 Teacher (as the Queen): Can anyone tell me how to get to the house where the gold miners live? I know they like apples!

| (17) Judging | Committing | Opportunity for control |

R23: They live in the woods.
R24: (*quickly*) They don't live there any more!
Q18: Are you sure?

| (18) Reasoning/ Creating | Committing | Opportunity for control |

R25: *They begin to talk among themselves—a mix of directions, misdirections, and discussions about whether they should or should not tell the merchant anything.*

Teacher Narration:

So the Queen found the path into the woods and came to the little house and knocked upon the door. And when Linda saw the enchanted apple, she bought the whole basket so that she could make a pie for her friends, the gold miners. But she could not resist taking a bite from an apple and no sooner did she taste the apple than she fell down upon the ground and was still.

The miners, returning home from work, passed through the village and heard the villagers talking about the visit of the apple seller.

Q19 Teacher (out of role): What stories did the villagers tell the miners?

(19) Recalling/ Creating	Committing	Opportunity for ownership

R26: They said an old woman came selling apples.
R27: And she wanted to know the way to your house!
Q20: Had anyone ever seen her before?

(20) Recalling/ Creating	Committing	Opportunity for control

R28: *A generous burst of information, including the fact that the old woman looked a lot like the Queen!*

Teacher Narration:

When they heard that, the miners hurried home only to find what they had feared. They saw Linda lying on the floor. They listened for her heartbeat but it was still; they checked to see if she was breathing, but nothing stirred. They laid her in a glass coffin and carried it to the woods.

And it came to pass that a King's son, whose name was Prince Emilio, was visiting from a faraway land and heard the story of the beautiful lady who lay in the woods.

Q21 Teacher (out of role): What do you think will happen now?

(21) Creating	Internalizing> Interpreting	Opportunity for control

Q22: How do you want the story to end?

(22) Creating	Interpreting	Opportunity for control

What the Teacher Is Promoting		
Knowing	Engagement	Controlling/ Owning

Teacher (out of role): Close your eyes or look down at your desk to help you think to yourself how you want the story to end. (*Quiet for slightly more than a minute.*)

Draw a picture which will show me what you think happened.

Q23: I wonder where you would put yourself in your picture?

(23) Creating/ Judging	Interpreting	Opportunity for control

R29: *The remaining class time is spent in working in crayon-resist. Much of the art is quite detailed and many of the students add writing to their pictures. The teacher notes that the students are much more interested in the content of one another's work than formerly. Although there is much moving about, it is mainly purposeful and non-aggressive.*

Session 2

In the morning, the teacher and students arrange the pictures on the wall, creating a picture gallery. All categories of both taxonomies are in play during this time as the students talk among themselves about the story, their parts in it, their pictures, and how these should be placed and why.

Towards the end of the discussion, rearranging, peer questioning, and admiring, one of the students asks the teacher this question:

Q24 (Student): I wonder what happened to her dad—he just sort of disappeared, didn't he?

(24) Solving	Interpreting	Demonstrating ownership

R30 (Teacher): I wonder, too.
They all look at the pictures thoughtfully.

Q25 (Teacher): Shall I read you the rest of the story of Linda this afternoon?

(25) Judging	Evaluating	Teacher hands over control

R31: Why?

Teacher: I thought you might like to hear someone else's ending to the story.

By their lack of enthusiasm, the teacher recognizes that the students are satisfied with their own work. I'll leave the story on the window shelf. Here are two other versions of the same story, as well, for you to look at and compare with your own.

Reflections on the use of two taxonomies

Knowing and learning are collective endeavours, processes that occur within the context of relationships with others.
—Linda Laidlaw (2005, p. 54)

In teaching, we should frame our questions to direct attention . . . from the "What's so?" to the "So what?" Only then will we get to the ultimate question we want students to ask of themselves: "Now what?"
—Thomas Estes and Dorothy Vasquesz-Levy (2001, p. 508)

The teacher, through her questions, has provided a lesson which has potential for capturing interest. She uses her storytelling techniques to make it easier for her students to listen and maintain interest.

By her use of role, she provides opportunities for using language spontaneously in a variety of ways in a non-pressured setting. Roles support the students' involvement with the material as well as giving them a strong measure of control over the teacher (e.g., as Queen). Role also allows this restless class to have reasons for moving about.

In this lesson, we see the teacher accepting and responding to her students' levels of engagement, but also offering opportunities for deepening involvement. The kinds of thinking demanded through questions are not tied to the sequential imperative of the taxonomy of knowing. However, a high degree of complex thinking comes from the students. In letting the students complete the story in their own ways, the teacher has allowed them to take control of the story and to have the satisfaction of interpreting an ending which has personal meaning for them. Despite her hope to have them compare their endings to that of the original fairy tale, she is prepared, in asking Question 25, to hand over the ownership of the material to her students—and they are willing to take it. The picture gallery activity enables them, through cooperative action and discussion, to see their work both as individual expressions and as a collective expression of response to the story.

When we examine the questions that the teacher asks, we see questions that tap into the students' backgrounds and experiences; that invite the students to contribute ideas and directions; that promote responses that come from the heart as well as the head; and that let the students, collectively, take over the story. What we don't see are many students engaged in question-asking. Question-asking, for these students, is inhibited both by their lack of skill with language and with their cultural perceptions of who has the right to ask the questions. Despite this, the teacher's questions do not exist in isolation—nor do her students' answers.

Questions have a wider purpose than as a means to a reply. They enable students to bring their own thoughts and feelings into expression either through answers or through their own questions. Teachers and students must learn to see questions not as hurdles to be got over, but as expressions of genuine interest that demand careful listening and thoughtful consideration. When this is understood, classroom discourse is vigorous and productive: questions and answers are woven together in the process of inquiry. The warp that holds the pattern of the discourse is made up of thought and feeling. Teachers' attention to providing diversity in ways of thinking and opportunities for engaging through many levels will enable their students to own their learning.

Any questions?

"You bet I have! I know I have to pay attention to feeling as well as to thinking and that questions shouldn't be tied to Bloom's taxonomy, but how do I make better questions? After all this theory, I need *practical* help."

Relax! That's what the next section is all about.

Chapter 5   A Classification of Questions

An education based upon
questions, understanding,
in-depth probing, and mastery of
disciplines is most likely to be
realized if it is not simply
described in the abstract.
—Howard Gardner (1999, p. 229)

Questions, like students, have an active role to play in the learning process. Some classifications of questioning identify their categories by type—for example, factual, conceptual, and contextual; here, we offer one classification that identifies a general *intention* for each category. Rather than asking, "What *type* of questions should I ask?" it is more practical to ask, "What do I want this question to *do?*"

The classification has three broad categories, each with a specific intention. We will outline these first and then go on to provide a series of source texts with examples.

A classification of questions by general function

These categories are taken from
and elaborate upon the original
classification given in Chapter 4 of
Morgan and Saxton, *Teaching
Drama: A mind of many wonders*
(1987).

Category A—Questions that elicit information: These questions draw out what is already known in terms of both information and experience and establish the appropriate procedures for the conduct of the work.

Category B—Questions that shape understanding: These questions help teachers and students fill in what lies between the facts and sort out, express, and elaborate how they are thinking and feeling about the material.

Category C—Questions that press for reflection: These questions demand intellectual and emotional commitment by challenging the individual to think critically and creatively.

Working from a different perspective, Brownlie, Close, and Wingren (1988) develop A. V. Manzo's ReQuest strategy for the teaching of reading. They suggest that students share with their teacher the responsibility for asking questions about their reading. In *Reaching for Higher Thought*, they offer a classification of questions which they identify as "on the line," "between the lines," and "beyond the lines." As with the three categories suggested here, these reading comprehension questions embody the same sense of *active* intention: Will this question have to do with what is already known? Will this question help us shape our understanding? Will this question make us think about the implications of what we are learning?

The functions of these categories are all equally important in the learning process, demanding different kinds of thinking. Research shows, though, that most questions asked in classrooms, whether by teachers or students, fall into Category A, eliciting information. If you want your students to think about what they are learning so that learning becomes part of their view of themselves and their world, you have to ask questions that will help them understand: questions that will connect them to the material (Category B) and help them think about the meanings being made (Category C).

These three categories reflect these principles:

- Students have the right to participate in their education and to be offered the means by which they can share responsibility for their learning.
- The collective nature of the classroom must be acknowledged. Students come to understand things by building joint frames of reference that enable them to participate in learning as a social and cultural process which is not "merely one of individual discovery but one of sharing, comparing, contrasting and arguing one's perspective against those of others" (Edwards and Mercer, 1987, p. 164).
- Every individual needs and has the right to be provoked into a consideration of ideas at the deepest levels of thought and feeling and must be given time for reflection. As Bruner (1986, p. 127) puts it, "Much of the process of education consists of being able to distance oneself in some way from what one knows by being able to reflect on one's knowledge."

Within every category, there is a range of questions, with each type serving a particular function. On the following pages, we offer some examples in order to show you the limitless possibilities of questions to mediate content, process, and investment.

Category A: Eliciting information—On the line

Category A covers six types of questions: questions that establish the rules of the game, questions that establish procedure, questions that establish or help control group discipline, questions that unify the class, questions that focus on recall of facts, and questions that supply information and may suggest implications.

1. Questions that establish the rules of the game

What do we need to remember so we don't get in the way of the work?
Function: A means of setting rules of behavior or reminding students of rules they have set previously

Can we manage without raising hands?
Function: To develop discussion skills by giving the students the responsibility for the ordering of the answers

What rules shall we make about latecomers?
Function: To guarantee the smooth operation of the class with minimum intrusion

First, there is the doing (process); then, the thinking on the doing (reflection). Finally, there is a redoing (process informed by reflection) that restarts these interactions again (13).

Process and reflection in any domain are sustained by and enrich the ability to think—and to think about thinking—that distinguishes us as human beings.
—Jessica Hoffmann Davis (2005, p. 17)

Category A questions are useful at any time in a lesson. They are a way for teachers and students to find out "what's up" quickly, to check knowledge, and set (or re-set) parameters.

Have you been listening?
Can everyone see?
Did anyone have trouble hearing Ted?
Can everyone hear?
Function: To ensure a good working atmosphere where individuals monitor the situation for themselves

2. Questions that establish procedure

Which order shall we go in?
Would it help if you talked this over with someone else?
How shall we re-form the groups?
Do you want to do this, or that?
Do we need to make a note of this?
Function: To help students consider the most productive ways for work

How are we going to do that?
Where should we do that?
How much time do you need?
How much *more* time do you need?
How can we do that more efficiently?
Function: To encourage students to develop skills in organizing time and space or method of work

Do we know enough to go on?
Have we enough material on which to base our conclusions?
What do we need to know now?
Can you manage on your own?
Function: To establish students' engagement in the material

Where can we find that information?
Who will be able to give us that information?
Function: To stimulate research

3. Questions that establish or help control group discipline

What size group will work best for you?
How will you arrange yourselves in the group?
Who will be responsible for keeping notes?
Who in the group has a watch?
How shall we arrange the desks?
Function: To help students work efficiently in groups independent of the teacher

4. Questions that unify the class

Are we all agreed that . . . ?
Are we ready to go on?
Has anyone anything to add?
Will you accept that for the moment?
Function: To ensure that the class can move along together

5. Questions that focus on recall of facts

What is the formula?
What were the terms of the will?
Could you summarize the main points so far?
What do we now know?
Function: To share facts in order to establish a firm foundation for further work

6. Questions that supply information and may suggest implications

With all the extra time it will require, are you still prepared to undertake the art display?
When the principal asks you to explain the arrangements, what will you say?
Function: To prepare students to deal with a possible challenge or to focus on the parameters of response

Often, the questions in Category A are closed; that is to say, they usually require yes, no, or other short answers. The examples above do not require a context because they deal with the operation of the lesson, whatever the material. In order to better understand Categories B and C, though, we have selected a number of sources that will not only clarify the thrust of the questions, we hope, but also be of interest to you.

Category B: Shaping understanding—Between the lines

Category B covers six types of questions: questions that reveal experience; questions that focus on making connections; questions that press students to rethink or restate by being more accurate and specific; questions that help promote expression of attitudes, biases, and points of view; questions that demand inference and interpretation; and questions that focus on meanings behind textual context.

1. Questions that reveal experience

A question I am asked often is this: "Is it cheating to use references?" In reply, I always quote Will Weng, one of my predecessors as *The Times* Crossword editor: "It's your puzzle. Solve it any way you want." And is it cheating to call The Times 900 number to get answers? Well, of course, but what nobody knows won't hurt you.
—Will Shortz (2001)

- *What sorts of ideas* do you have when you hear the phrase: "That's cheating!"?
- *What kinds of experiences* lead people to behave in that way?
- *What do you think* Mr. Shortz means when he says, "what nobody knows won't hurt you"?

Function: To discover what personal understandings students are bringing with them to the content of the lesson

In the examples that follow, we have italicized the words and phrases that can be transferred to other contexts.

Category B questions may invite participants to share what they know and what they feel about what they know; they are questions designed to connect individuals and the class as a whole to the material.

2. Questions that focus on making connections

When Canada was a very young country, people had little means of sending messages. Very rich people living in Quebec or Montreal sent private messengers from one place or the other to carry packets of letters to their friends. Sometimes people were lucky enough to persuade the Government courier to carry letters for them and, in spring when the hunters returned to Three Rivers, Montreal or Quebec, they also distributed news. Indeed, their homecoming was an event of great importance, if for no other reason than that they could give news of the settlers whom they had seen along the way, and could deliver messages entrusted to them.
—Moore and McEwen (1936, p. 76)

- *What connections are there between* this and the kind of thing that happens in our own lives?
- *How would it change* your lives if you were in a similar situation where communication was so apparently limited?
- *I wonder if people have always had and will always have* the same reactions as the settlers when communication is re-established?
- *What has this* source *to do with* the fact that the art of letter writing is dying out?
- *By what means* could the outposts communicate with the populated centres in an emergency?

Function: To require students to use what they know and apply it to the material at hand; to bring students today into a relationship with the past or the future

3. Questions that press students to rethink or restate by being more accurate and specific

I believe that the whole state of higher education is going to get worse. If my subject was flourishing and the universities were being treated in a more civilized way, it would be different . . .
—Simon Blackburn (1988)

- *What do you mean by* "civilized"?
- *How do you perceive* "it *would be* different"?
- *Can you put that in a way that* the general public would understand?

Function: To press for intellectual clarity when the meaning is veiled

Or

Everyone HATES Physics!
—A student, any day, any time, any year

- *What is it about your* Physics class *that makes you feel* so strongly?
- *Is it just* Physics *that* worries *you*?
- *I wonder what specific situation* might have triggered your reaction?

Function: To press for intellectual clarity when emotion clouds the meaning

4. Questions that help promote expression of attitudes, biases, and points of view

What does it say about progress when both source texts on this page are still relevant?

The Temagami wilderness controversy is smouldering like fire creeping through the undergrowth. After six months of increasing smoke, many of those involved warn that the confrontation over the Northern Ontario forest will erupt into an all-out blaze. The main question is not when it will start but who will start it.

Will it be the natives of the Teme-Augama Anishnabal (Deep Water People) who have vowed to continue their six-month blockade of access to a forest they say includes sacred grounds that are part of a larger, unresolved land claim?

Will it be the environmentalists, who are suing the province to protect a wilderness buffer around Lady Evelyn Smoothwater provincial park? The area is one of 76 threatened sites on a global register kept by the International Union for Conservation of Nature and Natural Resources, the world's largest alliance of conservation groups. Or will it be the loggers and town business leaders who have long claimed that the timber in the disputed area is vital to their economic survival?

The Temagami issue has often been painted as a north versus south struggle, pitting northern jobs and incomes against southern canoeists and tree worshippers. But wilderness outfitters also want the area saved, noting that about one-third of the Temagami economy depends on tourism untainted by the ravages of logging. . . . There are as many people in this area saying: "Save the wilderness" as there are saying: "Let them cut."
—Kathleen Kenna (1988)

- *Who would want to* be in the logging industry today?
- *Would you rather* preserve the environment and be unemployed or preserve your job and let nature look after itself?
- *Where do you stand* on this?
- As a citizen and a taxpayer, *what are your concerns?*
- *If it were* happening in your own backyard, *would you feel differently?*
- *Is it possible* to live in an area of conflict and not belong to any side?
- *How will* the inhabitants' perceptions of their world *be changed* by this controversy?

Function: To help develop attitudes to the area of study; to present opportunities for seeing material from a variety of viewpoints and to respect the attitudes and points of view of others; to become aware of the emotional power that is attached to ideas

5. Questions that demand inference and interpretation

Computers are a recent addition to the learning environment. They are useful in providing extensions of and support for science learning. They also help overcome restrictions of cost, time, accessibility and safety through simulations of expensive, time-consuming and dangerous activities. Computers should not, however, be regarded as a primary means of delivering science education or as a replacement for the direct investigation of natural and physical phenomena.
—Ontario Ministry of Education (1988)

- *How would you explain* to the people who hold the purse strings, that computers are an important and necessary adjunct to the science curriculum?
- *What might be implied by* the sentence, "Computers should not . . . be regarded as a primary means of delivering science education"?
- *How will* the Arts teachers perceive this expenditure?

Function: To require students to consider, justify, and explain textual statements, situations, or conclusions

6. Questions that focus on meanings behind textual content

A married couple in a Western state . . . ran a house of prostitution, using three older women whom they treated abominably. Then one Fourth of July they suddenly decided to give the "girls" a vacation, all expenses paid. Drove them to Yellowstone Park, treated them to a great time, and as they drove home to put the girls back to work, they said, "Girls, we appreciate your help," and the girls said, "Thanks."

Well, the Utah authorities arrested the couple for violating the Mann Act, bringing the women back across the state line for immoral purposes. Caught dead to rights, no contest, big fine and long prison sentences for the culprits . . . some judge wrote a most moving decision. Said the facts in the case were irrefutable, the Mann Act had been transgressed, a crime had been committed, and the punishment was not unreasonable. But, he added, sometimes the law hands down a judgment which offends the rule of common sense . . . the state could properly have arrested the couple at any time during the past dozen years for wrong that they were committing, but they waited until the pair was doing the right thing . . . bringing their girls back from a paid holiday. The sense of propriety on which society must rely had been offended. Case reversed. Couple set free.
—James Michener (1987, p. 173)

- *What is this* case really *about?*
- *What have we discovered about* judges and the law?
- *What place has* a sense of propriety in judgments that are, or should be, based on precedent?
- *Why do you think* the proprietors suddenly decided to give the "girls" a vacation?

Function: To probe for meanings essential to the understanding of the material

Category C: Pressing for reflection—Beyond the lines

Category C covers four types of questions: questions that develop suppositions or hypotheses, questions that focus on personal feelings, questions that focus on future action or projection, and questions that develop critical assessments or value judgments.

Category C questions press participants into deeper thought, into the kind of learning that considers any information as conditional upon its context, the possibility of a variety of perspectives, and the questions that lie therein.

1. Questions that develop suppositions or hypotheses

MAN BITES DOG!
—Newspaper headline

- I *wonder what* drove the man to bite the dog?
- I *wonder if* his wife will have to have him put down?
- *If* the dog was the main course, *what will* the man have for dessert?
- *Suppose* the man is discovered to be a veterinarian—*what then?*
- *What might* the neighbors be saying?

Function: To provide students with opportunities to think creatively about the facts. Here, the fact is a starting point and the questioner and responder may need to break the laws of logic.

2. Questions that focus on personal feelings

He saw clearly . . . how much it all meant to him, and the special value of some such anchorage in one's existence. He did not at all want to abandon the new life and its splendid spaces . . . and creep home and stay there. The . . . world was all too strong, it called to him still . . . and he knew he must return to the larger stage. But it was good to think he had this place to come back to, this place which was all his own, these things which were so glad to see him again and could always be counted upon for the same simple welcome.
—Kenneth Grahame (1908, p. 124)

- *Why is it that* you sometimes feel homesick even when you are at home?
- *What was in your mind* as you read this passage?
- *Is there* any place to which you would never return? *Why?*
- *What might be your concerns* as you prepare to move on to a "new stage" of your life?

Function: To give practice in the expression and sharing of personal feelings

3. Questions that focus on future action or projection

This poem, which has been edited for length here, is a wonderful piece of material with enormous appeal for students from about age 10 on.

Kill Ra: eat inside his head,
     see with his inside eye.
A cloud covers the moon: I nod my head
We to sleep again: she smiling.
At light, Ra and I to shore
     looking for broken branches waves sometides leave us.
I say, "go this way." He say, "No, that way."
Again he find, I nothing.
With stick Ra found, I kill him.
With pebble on beach, break his skull open,
Eat his soft eye.
I walk back slowly,
Now Ra faster than me.
I see picture of his woman saying why? why?
Now Ra's inner tongue tells me to say:
     "The waves took him."

My woman smiles. I sit in the sun.
Now with Ra's eye inside of me I see:
Night darker than darkness,
        darkness she cannot see.
—Ronald Duncan

- *What might happen when* he next searches for food?
- *How may* the last line *affect* his woman?
- *What are the consequences* for the three who are left?
- *Do* words like "salvation" and "punishment" *have any meaning* in a poem such as this?

Function: To look at implications of actions through conjecture; to experience cause and effect; to deal with what is as the basis for conjecture

4. Questions that develop critical assessment or value judgments

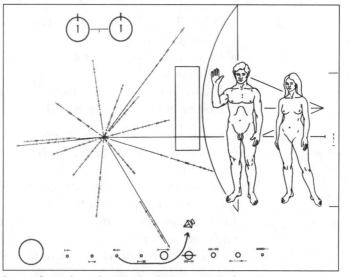

Image from the 6- by 9-inch plaque carried aboard a space probe, *Pioneer 10*

Is Anybody Out There?

For years astronomers have searched for evidence of intelligent life beyond our solar system. Since the short-lived US Project Ozma in 1960 radio telescopes have monitored hundreds of stars, though without picking up any noteworthy signals as yet. The US space probe, Pioneer 10, launched in 1972, used another approach: a plaque designed to communicate the language of science. The hydrogen atom (the most common element in the galaxy) is shown schematically at the top. The radiating lines of binary numbers below represent specific pulsars, arranged to show the position of our sun. The humans in front of the craft illustrate the kind of creatures that built it. At the bottom is our solar system, indicating which planet is ours
—Richard Marshall (1977, p. 50l)

- *How could you* design a plaque that more truly communicates life on our planet?
- *How can we justify* the amount of material we hurl into space?
- *Does it* really *matter* to you if there is life in outer space?

- *Where would you place the value of* the space program in relation to the needs of developing countries?

Function: To require students to look at their value systems; to find ways of balancing feelings with intellectual analysis

Flexible, non-hierarchical use of questions

These categories are *non-hierarchical.* You may introduce a question from any of the categories at any time during the lesson, depending on your objectives, your focus, and your students' needs, as well as what you want the question to *do.*

For example, as a means of attracting student interest, a History teacher may introduce a lesson on the causes of the Second World War with any of the following questions:

- How did Hitler justify his annexation of Sudetanland in 1938? (Category A)
- When might you be justified in taking over another country? (Category B)
- If you were an arms manufacturer, how would you feel about the possibility of war? (Category C)

Equally, any of these questions would be effective at other points in the lesson because they all deal with the teacher's major focus: Why do people go to war?

Education is a process of inquiry. Whether questions are used to further discussion, promote research, prompt summaries or reflection, focus the intelligence of the group, generate a collective emotional perspective, foster shared contexts and joint understandings, offer springboards to new knowledge, invite student participation, encourage talk, present different ways of communicating, or provide a means of handing over control and initiating ownership, they are the chief agents by which meanings are mediated.

Now let us look at a lesson to see how the classification operates through questions both in terms of categories and of functions.

Of the three ways of learning, instruction is the easiest to manage, the most orderly. Experience is the most powerful place to enter the cycle of [learning]. Uncovering what we know leads to the greatest change and forward movement.
—Eric Booth (1999, p. 197)

Chapter 6   The Example Lesson: Finding Areas

We have chosen a lesson in mathematics because students often have few opportunities for making decisions about such material and about the way in which the lesson is conducted. Typically, they also lack opportunity to contribute their own ideas.

This lesson on finding areas provides an alternative. On the left-hand side, we describe the progress of the lesson. On the right-hand side, we suggest the category—A, B, or C—and describe the particular function of the question. The lesson was taught in three sessions of about 40 minutes each.

Subject: Mathematics
Class: Grade 5 (11 years old)
Type: 28 students—boys
General Characteristics: The class shows a reluctance to sit still behind desks. Members resent what they see as routine work. When challenged, they exhibit lively, creative behavior. They have high self-esteem, bordering on arrogance.
Teacher's Objectives: To challenge students in such a way as to focus their energy on the problem through discovery for themselves; to forge a relationship between mathematics and their own lives
Math Objectives: To calculate area; determine and use formulae
Administration: 30 sheets of squared paper, extra rulers and pencils, 8 pieces of string (5 m in length) and 10 copies of map

"Q" followed by a number refers to a specific question raised most commonly by the teacher. "R" signifies a response to a question.

Session 1: Is there room for a football field?

	Category and Function
Ql: Are you ready to begin?	(A) Unifying class
Q2: Anyone need a pencil or a ruler?	(A) Establishing rules of the game
The teacher hands out squared paper. Generally, we don't do this until Grade 6 but I thought we'd have a stab at it.	Here the teacher is offering a challenge.

	Category and Function
Q3: Do you think you'll be able to manage? Rl: Sure!	(A) Suggesting implications The teacher knows they will go along but offers the challenge in order to engage their interest.
Teacher: The topic is areas, specifically of rectangles and, if that goes well, we shan't have any troubles with right-angled triangles.	
Q4: Where do you see a rectangle in this room? R2: (*Severally*) Doors, windows, desk tops, John's glasses, John's head . . .	(A) Establishing engagement The teacher acknowledges their testing of her by moving on quickly.
Teacher: Take the squared paper and, in the upper left-hand corner, draw a rectangle 3 squares long and 2 squares wide. *Students do so.*	
Q5: How many squares within the figure? R3: (*Severally*) Six squares.	(A) Recall
Q6: How many different-sized rectangles can you draw on the top half of your page? *Students draw.*	This instruction is masquerading as a question in order to add a little challenge to the task.
Q7: How many squares in your various rectangles? *Students count.*	(A) Recall
Q8: How many of your rectangles have the same number of squares as those of your neighbor? *Students consult.*	(A) Recall There is sharing in order to move along together.
Q9: What is the relationship between the length and width and the number of squares? R4: The number of squares is equal to the length times the width.	(B) Making connections
Q10: Is James right? Check it with your partner. *Teacher draws a rectangle 3 cm long and 5 cm wide.*	(A) Moving along together

Q11: If you agree that James is right, then what might be the formula for finding the area of this rectangle where A equals area, L equals length, and W equals width? R5: A equals L times W. Therefore, A equals 3 times 5 equals 15 cm.	(C) Developing hypothesis
Q12: Good. But what kind of centimetres are they? R6: They are *square* centimetres!	(C) Developing supposition
Q13: You bet! Now, what are the areas of a rectangle 8 cm long and 3 cm wide and a rectangle 12 cm long and 2 cm wide? R7: 24 square cm each.	(A) Recall
Q14: What does that tell you? R8: Different shapes can have the same areas.	(B) Making connections
The teacher has students test this out with a number of examples that they make up on their own.	
Q15: What are the measurements of a football field? R9: *Students tell her.*	(A) Recall
Q16: What . . . [is its area?] R10: *Students are already telling her the answer to the question she is about to ask.*	(A) Recall
Q17: We have 20 minutes left. In that time, can you find out whether the far field has an area large enough for a football field? Take a 5 m length of string and work in groups of four.	(A) Organizing time
Q18: Is there a watch in each group? R11: *Students check for watches as they find their groups.* When you get back there will be questions on the board for homework. R12: *Students rush off enthusiastically.*	(A) Establishing discipline

Homework questions on the chalkboard:

Q19: What is the area of the far field?	(A) Recall
Q20: Could you play a game of football on that area as it now is? Why or why not?	(B) Interpreting and inference
Q21: I own a piece of flat grassland whose area is larger than that of a football field. Why might it be unsuitable for football?	(B) Connecting, inferring, supposing

The class opens with a vigorous discussion about the homework questions and the teacher moves back into the lesson with Q22.

Session 2: Why does a farmer need to calculate areas?

Q22: What kinds of people need to calculate areas?
R13: Architects.

(A) Recall

Q23: Why would area measurement be important to an architect?
R14: My mother says that square footage is important in selling a house.
R15: And for selling land, too.

(B) Connecting, inferring

Q24: In what other ways would the area of land be important to, say, a farmer?
R16: Taxes.
R17: For the number of cows in his field.

(A) for some; (B) for others
Recalling, connecting, inferring

Q25 (student): Why would he need to know that?
R18: Because you can put only so many animals in a field.

(B) Making connections

Q26 (student): So? What's that mean?
R19: *There is a long silence. The teacher implies by her silence and her stance that she is prepared to wait because this is a question worth thinking about.*

(B) Making connections

Q27: Who would be able to tell us?
R20: She knows!

(A) Researching

Q28: Yes. Do you want me to tell you?
R21: *They nod!*
It has something to do with eating.
R22: *Students discuss in groups and come up with the answer: every cow has to have so much land on which to graze.*
Teacher: Well done! I don't know about cows, but I do know that one sheep in southern Ontario needs 1000 square m for maximum health.

(A) Deciding procedure

Q29: How many sheep could we run on the far field?
R23: *Students calculate and come to an agreement.*

(B) Connecting

Q30: If we want to reseed the far field, what will we need to know?
R24: *A general discussion allows the teacher to assess whether the class is ready to move on.*

(C) Supposing

Preparation for the next class: On the chalkboard the teacher draws a series of figures which she then covers.

Homework

Q31: How can you find the area of a right-angled triangle which has a height of 5 cm and a base of 4 cm?

(B) Connecting

Q32: Bill, will you find out from your uncle the amount of land required for a cow?

(A) Supplying information Question for Bill's uncle, but for Bill it is an instruction in the guise of a question.

Session 3: How can settlers ensure that land is divided fairly?

Bill brings in the information that was requested in the previous class and a brief discussion and comparison result. The teacher then asks the students to compare their homework with each other and to deduce the formula for a right-angled triangle. She asks Q33.

Q33: How did you go about finding that out?
R25: I made it into a rectangle and found the two halves were the same.
R26: I asked my brother.

(A) Recalling, unifying

The teacher then gives several right-angled triangles for them to calculate area to ensure that everyone understands the principle.

Q34: How can we use our knowledge of the areas of rectangles and right-angled triangles to find the areas of the figures on the board?
She reveals the board.

(B) Connecting

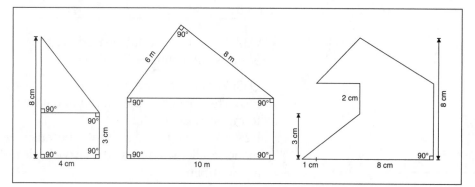

Students work in pairs and check their answers with the teacher.
Teacher: We are now going to work differently. You are a group of settlers who have been granted a large parcel of land. Together you have cleared the land. All of us have worked hard and long.

Notice how the teacher joins the class by her use of the words "we" and "us."

Q35: How could we ensure that the land we have been allotted is divided fairly amongst our seven families?
Teacher (continuing):
In those days, they had different scales of measurement from those we use today but, for our purposes, I think it would be more useful to stick with the metric system.

(B) Connecting;
(C) Critically assessing

Q36: Would it help if you worked in family groups, or would you rather work individually?
Students decide to work in family groups and are given maps of the land parcel.

(A) Establishing procedure

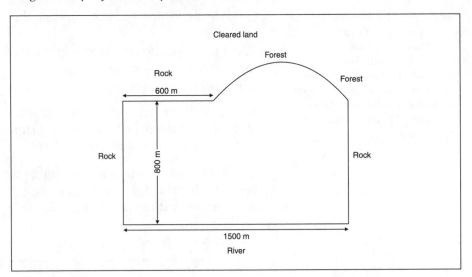

Q37: What is the total cleared area?
She gets many different answers.

(A) Sharing facts

Q38: Why do our answers vary?
R27: The curves in the map make it hard to measure accurately.
R28: Ours is more accurate because we made smaller squares so the curve is almost a straight line.

(B) Interpreting

Students eventually agree on a figure for the total area.
Q39: We are seven families. How much land should the families receive if there is a fair distribution?
Students work it out to the nearest square metre by dividing the total area by seven.

(B) Connecting

Q40: Now that we know how much every family is entitled to, how shall we split this land into equal parts? R29: We could try it and then count the squares.	(B) Connecting
Q41: Do you still want to work in families? R30: *Students agree that it is most enjoyable to work in families except for one boy who complains that he is doing all the work.*	(A) Considering ways to work
Q42: I wonder if that same complaint would have been made in earlier times? R31: *The students carry out the task and are able to find seven approximately equal lots of land, which satisfies the teacher's math objective.*	(B) Connecting
Q43: I wonder how the family who drew Lot C will water their cattle? R32: *This rhetorical question is not expected to draw any answers, but rather, to set the students into reflecting on the difficulties of making a fair distribution of land.*	(C) Projecting

There is more to land than square metres, so the teacher's final question is a "thinker" question.

Reflections on the lesson

There is no doubt that in these lessons the teacher wanted her students to learn how to calculate areas and use formulae. There is no doubt, either, that she could have taught all that in one lesson; she could have presented the formulae and allowed the students to practise them. She would then be able to discover, by testing, how many students had taken in the material and were able to hand it back to her and apply it in different ways.

It is doubtful, though, whether the majority of students would have the kind of understanding of the principles of the formulae that these students have—even many years later, they remember that series of lessons and, what is more, have no difficulty in determining areas! We suggest that, as can be seen through her questioning, the teacher understood the importance of taking the time to put her students into the material, as well as to bring the material to them.

How did the teacher bring the material to her students?

- She captured their interest.
- She provided them with tasks that engaged them with the material.
- She varied the pace, making the social health of the class work for her, rather than against her.

- She invited with questions rather than ordering through instructions.
- She gave many opportunities for students to make decisions about the way in which they learned.
- She was honest about what was to be learned.

How did the teacher put her students into the material?

- She took the time for the students to discover for themselves.
- She used a variety of strategies and techniques to create a personal framework for the students.
- Through her teaching, the validity and purpose of the lesson material were proven, not for the students by her, but *by them for themselves.*
- The way in which the teacher structured the questions challenged the students at all levels of competence to think about the material and the situations or problems she set up. The questions permitted the students to exercise their feelings as they manipulated the material.
- The teacher offered many opportunities for ownership and for taking control through shared activities and peer teaching.

In summary, here is a teacher who uses the Taxonomy of Personal Engagement as a guide for bringing the material to her students; who is prepared to make the time to allow students to find their own relationship with the material; and who enables them to think and feel in many different ways by using all the categories of questions.

You may have noticed that the last question the teacher asks is identified as a "thinker" question. Questions can be defined in many ways. In the next chapter, we provide a glossary of questions: knowing the definitions will enable a more flexible repertoire of questions.

According to Jerome Bruner (1996, p. 84), human learning is at its best "when it is participatory, proactive, communal, collaborative, and given over to constructing meanings rather than receiving them."

Chapter 7   A Glossary of Questions

According to John Ralston Saul, we are at our best when we "concentrate on questioning and clarifying and avoid the specialists' obsession with solutions" (1993, p. 576).

Definitions, like questions and metaphors are instruments of thinking. Their authority rests entirely on their usefulness, not their correctness.
—Neil Postman (1979, p. 145)

In any reading you have done or in any course you may have taken about teaching, you will probably have been warned against using one kind of question and encouraged to use another kind. People will stress the importance of the divergent question. Professor X will tell (or has told) you never to use the covert question. Doctor Y says that covert questions are the key to discovery learning and everyone agrees that the key to effective questioning is the use of the key question!

Many questions have different names for the same or similar functions—the heuristic, the creative, and the freeing, for example—and some names are umbrellas: for example, the open question covers such questions as the reflective, the divergent, and the hypothetical. You may know different names for the questions we will describe because you have read different books and been taught by different teachers. There is a staggering breadth of terminology and we have selected some 50 terms for definition. The order is designed to maintain your interest and not to suggest a hierarchical approach.

From higher-order to unanswerable questions

Higher-order questions are those that ask for analysis, synthesis, or evaluation, the last three categories of Bloom's taxonomy. According to the taxonomy, these demand more complex and thus higher levels of thinking. For example:

Analysis:

> Why is it so important for different cultural groups in our society to maintain their cultural heritage?

Synthesis:

> For the end-of-the-year concert, what theme could we look at that would best express the wide variety of cultures in our school?

Evaluation:

> What significance has the government's decision to opt for the concept of the *cultural mosaic* over that of the *melting pot* for today's society?

Lower-order questions are those that ask for knowledge, comprehension, and application, the first three categories of Bloom's taxonomy. According to the taxonomy, these demand less complex and thus lower levels of thinking. For example:

Knowledge:
How many different cultural groups are represented in our classroom?

Comprehension:
What do we mean by the *cultural mosaic*?

Application:
What other examples of cultural policy promote social ghettoization?

The **closed question** is of two main varieties:

(a) It asks for a short, right answer:

What was the political system in Germany in 1933–45?

(b) It may be answered by "yes" or "no" and can be recognized by the use of the interrogative structure of verb-noun, for example, "Is it?" "Have you?" "Will you?" "Shall we?":

Have you done your homework?

Note that Categories B and C are not well served by the closed question and that for anything further to happen, another question has to be posed. The closed question is useful for testing recall, focusing attention, obtaining information, and for moving on quickly when you wish to avoid discussion. It is often a way of helping reluctant students into talk because it does not ask them to put anything of themselves into the answer.

On the other hand, the **open question** suggests that the teacher does not have one particular answer in mind, but is inviting students to consider and advance many possibilities. This kind of question is "open" to many answers:

What kinds of things can the government do for the homeless?

Overt and covert questions are designed to elicit feeling responses. The **overt question** is direct and generally produces a short answer. It can sometimes be seen as threatening. Examples:

How are you feeling?
Were you afraid?
Would you like to . . . ?
Why didn't you do your homework?

The **covert question** is indirect and invites elaboration; it often masquerades as a statement:

What is in your mind?
What are your concerns?
How might one describe that experience?
It must be difficult to hold a job and keep up with your schoolwork?

It is useful to remember that closed and open questions influence the *length* of the responses: open questions ask for responses of greater length while closed questions tend to limit contributions.

The **polar question** asks a question to which the answer must either be yes or no, true or false. It is used extensively in questionnaires that are designed to polarize or unify opinion; there is no chance to respond with "maybe," "sometimes," or "it depends." Example:

Is butter bad for you?

The **branching question** gives students a choice between alternatives:

Shall we do this . . . or that . . . ?
Will it be either . . . or . . . ?
Shall we get help or try it on our own?

The **confrontation,** or **"tough,"** **question** attempts to eliminate inconsistency and challenges the validity of what has been said or done. Graves (1983) suggests that such a question causes in the student "a temporary loss of control" because it challenges the validity of what he has been engaged upon or the logic of what he has been saying (or writing); however, you should still challenge a student's thinking when the need for clarification arises:

A few minutes ago you said that the Native peoples of northern Quebec should have sole rights over their territories and now you say that Quebec Hydro should be allowed to build dams there. How do you explain this contradiction?

The **key question**, also known as the *critical question* or the *driving question*, opens up the issue:

I wonder if it matters that students with learning disabilities learn little in the integrated classroom, provided they have the social experience?

For Miller and Saxton (2004b), key questions lie at the heart of the content material. They provide for "the direction of the lesson and the reference points for reflection" (p. 6). This example comes from page 100:

What is the relationship between a good education and a good human being?

The characteristics of deductive and inductive questions need to be clearly understood. Common understanding is that if the question is *deductive*, the statement in the question has to be accepted and the answerers' job is to prove it:

Cinderella is a classic fairy tale. What are the characteristics of a fairy tale?

If the question is *inductive*, the answerer will have to look at a series of instances and encompass them in an answer:

What are the characteristics of a classic fairy tale?

We often teach through the deductive process without realizing its implications. How many adults think of Hamlet only as a man who couldn't make up his mind? Deductive reasoning can be limiting because all you will be looking for in Shakespeare's text is where it supports or refutes that opinion; the chances are that you will overlook the other aspects of Hamlet's character which might cause you to think very differently about him. On the other hand, by asking, "What kind of man was Hamlet?" the student can bring his experiences and his feelings, as well as his knowledge of the text, into an answer. That's more difficult to assess, of course!

Let us clarify the differences. The **deductive question** confines the area of inquiry. It is, as Weingartner (1977, pp. 12–14) points out, reductive and convergent; it narrows down the possibilities. The **inductive question** widens the process of inquiry. It is expansive and divergent; it offers a panorama of possibilities. If, as Hunkins (1974, p. 9) says, "inductive and deductive thinking are complementary parts of a continuous cognitive process," then it becomes important to know which you are using and why you are using it.

Questions that require a written reply tend to be deductive rather than inductive because the answers are easier to assess. The questions confine the area. They must be carefully planned because you won't be there to rephrase if they are ambiguous. Written questions usually follow the statement–question format:

> Caesar was said to be ambitious. What evidence in Shakespeare's *Julius Caesar* do you have to support or refute this statement?

The **heuristic**, or **creative, question** guides the student into discovering the answer for himself through all his resources—knowledge, experience, imagination, and feelings:

> Now that we all know the facts about our situation, what are the implications for each one of us?

The **educative**, or **productive, question** is designed to help students learn, leading them to new facts, new perspectives, and new ideas:

> If we were to be part of an expedition to a new planet, what kind of people would we need to be?

The **freeing question** is one where the teacher clearly signals that there is no one right answer; the student is free to wonder:

> I wonder what happened to unicorns?
> (Our favorite answer: "Only one got into the Ark.")

The **hypothetical question** is one that frees responders to let their imaginations run wild. For example, consider this favorite essay topic among 10- to 14-year-olds:

> What would you do with a million dollars?

Note that although this question demands a creative response, it can sometimes cause problems. If the question lacks a focus, it can produce unstructured and unfocused answers. You might try this question instead:

> How would you spend a bequest of a million dollars and for whose benefit?

The **divergent question** invites many different responses from a large number of students and encourages both concrete and abstract thinking:

What might happen in a hospital if the water system became contaminated?

The **factual question** requires students to give information:

How is oxygen absorbed by the blood?

The **recall question** asks a student to draw from his knowledge or experience. This type of question is the most popular/infamous and ubiquitous question in the teaching lexicon:

What did Margaret just say, Duncan?
What is a right-angled triangle?

The **research question** not only invites the students into research, but also invites them to assume responsibility for designing the procedure for the research:

How could we find out how to measure the weight of the earth?

The **probing question** asks students to think more deeply about the reasons they hold certain assumptions:

I wonder if you could tell us a little more about why you think that might be a problem?

The **enactive question** drives the responder into further thought and possibly direct action:

What are we going to do about it?

The **social question** is so-called because it is used as part of classroom management and as a means of pulling the group together:

Aren't we straying beyond the point?

The **rhetorical question** is designed to affect feeling and thought; no answer is expected:

Who among you has not sinned? (Guilt) Who cares? (Deflation)

The **thinker question** is one that, like the rhetorical, evokes feeling and thought and does not require an answer. It is generally asked at the end of the lesson in the hope that students will think about it before the next lesson. It is often prefaced with the phrase "I wonder . . . ?" or "Do you suppose that . . . ?":

I wonder how the family who drew Lot C will water their cattle?

The **reflective question** clearly signals that an immediate answer is not required; that the teacher is prepared to wait; that it is acceptable to think aloud and there need be neither a resolution nor a consensus:

Can you remember a time when your future depended upon someone you didn't trust?

The *opening question*, a term coined by Graves (1983), is not to be confused with the open question. **Opening questions** are designed to open up dialogue between teacher and student(s). They have to do with the teacher's ability to recognize student mood in order to promote engagement with the work:

> How is it going, Ted?
> Interesting work. What are all of you intending to do now?

The **following question** (Graves, 1983) is also known as the *mirror question* (Brooks and Emmert, 1976). It reflects what has just been said by the student in order to help him hear what he has just said:

> Student: We should stop letting foreigners into our country.
> Teacher: You think that we should keep all foreigners out?

The intention here is the implied question, "Are you saying . . . ?" Try to avoid correcting, changing the language, or infusing your own biases by your tone of voice. This "mirroring" technique, as Graves (1983) calls it, is used extensively in counselling.

The **synopsis question**, also called the *review* or *summary question*, is designed to help students crystallize their thinking up to a certain point:

> Where did we get to yesterday?
> What are the important points to come out of this discussion?

The **clarifying question** invites the student to elaborate a somewhat bald statement, to refine a rather "woolly" comment (or, at any rate, one that you don't understand!):

> Can you be more specific?
> I wonder why you might think that?
> I don't quite understand what you mean. Perhaps someone else could help me?
> I wonder if there is another way you could put that?
> Am I right in thinking . . . ?

The **process**, or **development, question** is that question which asks the student to look at the steps from the beginning of the task to arrive where he is presently, in order to help him discover for himself where he should go next or for him to see how a particular activity has helped him to move forward:

> What have you been doing up 'til now?
> Let's look at how you got this far?

The **evaluating question** invites students to look at their work in a critical fashion:

> What did you learn from this?
> What new skills have you acquired?
> How does this compare with your work last term?
> How valid are our conclusions?

The **silly question** is that question which is not asked because the person who would like to ask it worries about looking silly. If you need to know something, though, you are silly not to ask the question that will help you to find out!

The **"stupid" question** is that question which someone has the courage to ask, but lacks confidence in doing so. It is generally prefaced by the phrase "I know I sound stupid, but . . . "

There is another kind of "stupid" question, too: the question that has such a simple and obvious answer that students can't believe their teacher is asking it. While they search madly for some other answer, the teacher is left wondering why the question is so difficult for them. It is only later that the teacher may realize that she was asking a "stupid" question and the students were too polite to tell her that!

Watch any courtroom drama on TV to discover how a leading question is used and how often the lawyers get away with it.

In the **leading question**, the question tells, strongly implies, or prompts the answer that is being sought. Most often, it uses the closed structure:

> Would you not say that the fog made it difficult for an accurate identification of the alleged assailant?

Leading questions can also be used to check for understanding or to see if a student is fully committed:

> You agree, then, that we should be more careful in how we tell them that they are wrong?

A **loaded question** operates to touch the feelings in such a way that the student is caught in a dilemma from which it is difficult to escape. As the descriptor indicates, loaded questions carry heavy emotional weight and are designed to deepen thought. As challenges, they should be used carefully:

> I wonder, then, just what is your definition of patriotism?

The **serialized**, or **machine gun**, **question** gives the student no opportunity to think independently before alternatives are thrust at him:

> If you were going to university, would you enroll at Queen's? How about York? Or Western? Or Simon Fraser?

Often, a question becomes a marathon because the asker is anxious to offer as much help as possible. Anyone who has attended or been questioned at an oral defence for a higher degree will recognize the marathon question.

The **marathon question** is long and involved, and students often lose the thread. This may be because the questioner has not fully thought out how to construct the question and is trying desperately to make sure that there *is* a thread:

> What do you think we should do about free trade—keep out competition from other countries by raising tariffs on their produce, even if this means we don't have as much foreign trade—or try to increase our trade with other countries by agreeing with them to lower our tariffs if they lower theirs?

The **ambiguous question** is one that leaves the student unsure of what to reply to or how his answer, if he has one, will be interpreted. The main part of the question is often followed by "or not":

> Do you think Canada should supply arms to Third World countries or not?

If the student says, "yes," does he mean "Yes, I think we should," or "Yes, I think we shouldn't"? This question is closed. Tagging on "or not" does not make it open, just impossible to answer (although students will still try).

The **double-barrelled question** is one where a bias (generally subconscious) intrudes on the question:

> Which story appeals to you: one that is short and well written or one that is long and frivolous?

Your students may prefer something short and frivolous!

The **prompt**, or **elicitation**, **question** is accompanied by heavy clues which are to be found in the wording of the question, the intonation, or the pauses to be filled in by students:

> This is a . . . ?
> The knife is . . . [sharp, indrawn breath] . . . ?
> We should remember to be . . . ? . . . when we are using knives.

Edwards and Mercer (1987, p. 105) warn us that the problem with questions like this is "that they can give a false impression [to the teacher] of the extent to which the students [really] understand what they are saying and doing."

Here is a demonstration of a **contrapuntal question**:

> James, you remember that experiment, the one I was referring to, not the one in January—that was a mistake on my part—the one in February, the experiment which is referred to in your text? You know the one I'm talking about, there's no mistake about it, is there? Now, during that experiment there were three of you present—you, Pam, Ricky and Leslie—no, that makes four, I'm sorry. There were four people present and what I want to ask you, James, is did any of you during that experiment—any one or more of you, I mean you or Pam or Rick or Leslie—I think there was no one else present. Now, James, this is very important, I shall make a note of your answer, did you, or Pam or Rick or Leslie—anyone of you, I mean—write anything like this? I don't mean the actual words—no one expects you to remember the exact words all that time ago, but anything of the kind, I mean? I'm waiting for your answer, James.

Need we say anything more?

A common, but sometimes controversial question is the **why question**. Many educators and most psychologists suggest that *why* questions should be avoided. In part, we agree when these can be perceived as a tool to destroy confidence or to suggest disapproval, objections, or criticism:

> Why would you say that? (prying into personal life)
> Why did you do that? (criticizing personal choice)
> Why do you always wear that color? (attacking the way someone presents self)

Dillon (1983, pp. 30–31) suggests "from long experience, children have learned that there is, in fact, no meaningful answer to a 'why' question." Consider, for example:

Where there is no choice, questions are irrelevant. "Why?" is not the word that springs to the lips of the man in a shell-hole pulling a corpse onto himself for cover.
—Pauline Holdstock (2004, p. 109)

"I like this book a lot," a child would say, the teacher would reply, "Did you? Why?" and the answer would very often be a sigh or a look of pain or shrugged shoulders or a puzzled frown . . . [Why] is a catch-all question, too big to answer all at once. No one can explain in a couple of sentences why s/he liked or disliked a book. That's the reason children use catch-all words in reply: it was exciting, it was fun; it was boring, it was dull.
—Aidan Chambers (1996, p. 41)

Why haven't you done your homework?

The student knows that the questioner is not interested in the answer, but is using the question as a means to inform the student of her displeasure or frustration.

On the other hand, *why* is the great educational question. It is the way in which we learn—it drives us to discover our world. We all ask why questions but it is *the way* in which a why question is asked and the tone that changes it from a perceived personal interrogation of the respondent to being seen as a genuine need to know on the part of the questioner.

A *why* question can be softened with the addition of "I wonder" before the word "why."

The **everyday question** is one that comes readily to mind. It often springs thoughtlessly from the lips as part of a kind of ritual dialogue which serves a social function and often does not expect or get an answer (or at least a detailed answer!):

How are you?
What have you been doing?
What have I done with my glasses?

Sometimes, it seemed to me that I spent my days asking questions, trying to fit together the pieces of the puzzle whose edges were ever-expanding . . . "There is a moment," Jacques had observed, "when you have to let go, to stop asking why, because it's just like that. Even we can't explain why things are the way they are too well sometimes, except to say, that's the way it is. It's in our customs, our culture. Some questions have no answers."
—Michael Sanders (2002, p. 287)

And then there are **unanswerable** or **eternal questions** of existence: Who am I? Why am I here? What is truth?

These are some of the "**essential questions**" that Gardner (1999) lists in *The Disciplined Mind.* They are the questions of the very young child, posed most often "in the language of fairy tales, myths and pretend play"(p. 216), but they are also questions of tremendous interest to adolescents and are usually initiated by them when the context is right. It is a signal to those questioned of an ability and a need to reason in abstractions.

Northrop Frye (1988, p. 192) writes, "Heidigger says the first question of philosophy, and the hardest to answer because it's also the simplest, is: 'Why is there something rather than nothing?'"

Before we leave these definitions of question terminology, there is one other term with which you should be familiar: *recitation.* The term has nothing to do with reciting a poem, such as "La Belle Dame Sans Merci." It is a classroom procedure in which "the teacher asks a question, the student gives an answer, the teacher evaluates the answer, and in the same breath, asks another question" (Dillon, 1988b, p. 85). In this procedure the teacher controls the discourse, little time is given for considering the answers (your own and others), and the constant evaluation of answers is extremely inhibiting. *We most strongly urge you to avoid this procedure.* There is one more caution: certain teacher questions would be dangerous for the student to answer. Consider, for example:

How many times have I told you that?

Alternatives to questions

Ardith Cole (2002, p. 16) describes some statements as "inside-out questions" that need to be considered in the same way as questions.

You will have noticed that some of the sample questions used in earlier chapters look more like statements than they do questions. Statements often take the place of questions and are valuable additions to a questioning repertoire. They work extremely well, providing that students understand that a statement is offered as an invitation for discussion. Cole (2002) points out that elementary students who have little experience with statements can become confused, as they tend to see a statement as something that cannot be disputed.

A **declarative statement** is used to express a thought and to generate an exploration of that thought. It conveys information and it does not prescribe what kind and how much response is expected:

> I see no reason why 15-year-olds can't be recruited to fight for their country.

Studies "suggest that responses to teacher statements may be both longer and more complex than responses to questions."
—J. T. Dillon (1988b, p. 137)

A **reflective restatement** is used to summarize and synthesize what a speaker has just said. It can be used to encourage a student to elaborate upon his original contribution, and as a way of suggesting that, if there is a misunderstanding, it is on the part of the listener rather than inadequacy or confusion on the part of the speaker. Barbara Hill (personal communication, May 26, 2006) notes that a reflective restatement is useful in parent–teacher interviews to ensure correct understanding before proceeding. It conveys to parents that the teacher is listening and taking parent remarks seriously.

A reflective restatement often begins with phrases such as these: "I understand you to say that . . . " "You mean that . . . " "What you are saying is . . . "

Note the teacher's reflective restatement in this exchange:

> Student: Well, like it seems to me that . . . , I mean there are some things that people shouldn't be allowed to pass on—like this friend of mine who got a kind of blood poisoning in hospital, you know . . . ?
> Teacher: You are saying that we need more efficient ways of analysing blood.
> Student: Well, maybe. But what I was really meaning was that people with these kinds of diseases should be put away.

This teacher's reflective restatement enabled the student to clarify for himself and for the teacher and the class what it was he really meant, which led to a lively discussion indeed!

A **state of mind statement** is used to express a state of mind or feeling. It often begins with phrases such as the following: "I'm not sure I am coping with . . ." "I don't feel comfortable with . . ." "I'm not sure I know enough about . . ." It allows students to see that the teacher is human and suffers from the same confusions and difficulties as they do. Most important, it removes the teacher from being the one who always *can* to being the one who sometimes *can't*. It invites students to elaborate, to help, even to direct.

An **invitational statement** is used to invite a student to elaborate. It is often prefaced with such phrases as "I'd like to hear more about . . . " or "I'd be interested in knowing . . . " An invitational statement demonstrates the teacher's personal interest in a student's contribution. It is most effective on a one-to-one basis because it gives value to what the student has said as well as the experience that prompted it.

And then there is always "the other way around."

- The *question that should be a statement:* "Don't you think it would be helpful if you studied more?" is really the statement "You'd get higher marks if you studied more."
- The *instruction that masquerades as a question:* "Shall we get into groups of four?"

These kinds of question-statements or question-instructions are often used when a teacher wants to appear democratic instead of authoritative. They are widely used by teachers who are anxious for student approval of their instructions. Have they ever thought of the consequences if the students said, "No!" out loud? "Groups of four, please" is faster, cleaner and more to the point!

What's in a name?

In Chapter 5 we presented a classification of questions made up of three categories. Each category had a function—*eliciting information* (Category A), *shaping understanding* (Category B), and *pressing for reflection* (Category C)—and each general function had several particular functions.

A function can be performed by many tools. For example, a screwdriver and a penny can both open something. So, too, there are many kinds of questions for every category. Every time you plan or ask a question, it is unnecessary for you to identify that question by name, but knowing the names of questions and what they do will make it easier to analyse your questions and those of others and help your students understand and use them. Whatever the question you ask, whatever its kind and function, the first guide in asking questions is to think about *how the question will help students engage in and with the material.*

Questions do not operate in a vacuum. You and your students need to work with an open agenda, where they see their relationship with you as collaborative and teaching as an attempt to negotiate shared meanings and understandings (Edwards and Westgate, 1987). It is often a long process to arrive at the point where students accept that without their contributions, the work cannot proceed; that the teacher is prepared to wait for answers because she recognizes that questions need to be considered and that thoughtful answers need time for formulation.

In Chapter 8, we set that context by looking at the characteristics of effective classroom interaction: the nature of classroom talk, the characteristics of classroom discourse, and the power of "active" silence.

Chapter 8 Fewer Questions, Better Questions, and Time to Think

To conceive an educative question
requires thought;
To formulate it requires labour;
To pose it, tact.
None of this is mysterious
And all of it is within our reach.
—J. T. Dillon (1983, p. 8)

We are by nature question-asking,
answer-making, problem-solving
animals and we are extremely
good at it, above all when we are
little.
—John Holt (1982, p. 189)

There is a need to be interested in
the ideas and creations of one's
own time. To read, to think, to ask
questions and to talk in wide
circles, well beyond any particular
competence.
—John Ralston Saul (1993, p. 110)

The classic concept of learning is that it occurs when the teacher asks the questions and the students can answer them; the reality is that learning does not occur until learners need to know and can formulate the question for themselves.

We must recognize that however indispensable as teachers we consider ourselves, children have been learning by themselves and asking questions since they were born. We must not allow our students to lose this natural ability by ignoring it. Classroom interaction is the activity that sets students into the process of inquiry—thinking, feeling, discussing, arguing, philosophizing, and more—and the teacher is, most often, the initiator of the action.

The teacher, Vygotsky and Bruner suggest, is central as a guide to effective learning (Bruner, 1986). The job of the teacher is to open doors: to let students know that doors exist, that there are many doors, that they are meant to be opened (some easily, some with difficulty), and that beyond every door there is something worth knowing. The key to the door, to carry the analogy further is, most often, the "good" question.

When something is put into words, it promotes control of the knowledge that is expressed. As Woods (1987) suggests, speaking those words can be the "essential moment of appropriation and re-interpretation which helps establish ownership." Questioning generates the kind of talk and communication that can lead to learning; questioning reveals to the teacher the readiness of students to take control; and questioning by both students and teacher establishes the communicative nature of the classroom. And it is the nature of the discourse that dictates the quality of the learning.

Classroom discourse—Talking in wide circles

The basic difference between many people engaged in social conversation and students engaged in traditional educational discourse is one of organization.

When we engage in free-flowing conversation in a social situation, we talk in pairs or in small groups, and these groupings dissolve and re-form as the topics of conversation develop or change. Our interest in the content controls the organization.

Discourse is informal. It has a flexible structure and generally is centred on a topic or theme; it is inconclusive in nature, although points for further investigation can be identified. (See Appendix 1 for more.)

In the classroom, our conversations embrace everyone in the class at the same time. In order to maintain a focus, to ensure that everyone has a chance to contribute (the silent to be jogged into speech, the verbose to be eased into silence), we need someone to take control and 99 per cent of the time, that someone is the teacher. The effect is to put the teacher at the centre of the conversation: everything passes through the teacher and students expect everything to be mediated by the teacher. There is nothing wrong with this when it is important for everyone to share a common basis of information or when the teacher wants to assess how much the students know; however, it is not the kind of classroom discourse we are talking about here.

In a communicative classroom, students are expected to contribute and the way in which the talk is advanced draws directly on their background, experiences, and prior knowledge. Against these frames of reference, the new information is assessed—"What's that got to do with me?"—and measured—"How important is that to me?—and through them, new information and experience can be absorbed, internalized, and owned.

Students need to understand the correspondence between questions and answers: some questions evoke what Cole (2002) describes as a "rich response" while others require "more easily located, surface details." These different types of questions Cole calls "thin" and "thick." *Thick questions* call on us to "crawl down between the lines" and make connections with our own experiences (p. 49) and, as we know, the longest-lasting learning occurs when personal experience and new ideas are brought together.

As early as 1958, research was demonstrating that a knowledge of students' backgrounds made a "significant difference in a teacher's effectiveness as measured by students' learning" (McKeachie, 1978, p. 38). Productive classroom discourse gives students opportunities to make connections with their own lives and to be responsible for the organization of that discourse (who speaks and when, who asks questions, and so on). "This important mode of learning," as Britton (1970) refers to it, allows them to help control what ideas are introduced and developed. (For an analysis of talk, discourse, and discussion, see Appendix 1.)

Participants profit from their own talking . . . from what others contribute and, above all, from the interaction—that is to say, from the enabling effect of each upon the others.
—James Britton (1970, pp. 239–40)

Characteristics of effective classroom discourse

It takes time to promote effective classroom discourse. Be sure to consider the following in establishing a climate for it.

1 Thought shapes language and language shapes thought, and both are necessary in the cognitive, social, and emotional development of students. Talk is a way of sorting out ideas. Discourse is a valuable way to sort, depending, as it does, upon the gradual accumulation of shared contexts of talk and experience. Out of their shared contexts, students build "joint frames of reference" (Edwards and Mercer, 1987, p. 65).

2 Discourse can give students practice in making questions and assessing their impact. It should be an opportunity for them to control and direct the exchange of ideas. Within the larger discourse, small

"Scaffolding" is Bruner's term for one of the principles of Vygotsky's theory of intellectual development and best describes what it is that goes on when teaching and learning come together in joint activity; that "zone" where learning is neither "student-centred" nor "teacher-centred," but centred in what happens between them; where students' potentials are realized because of teacher guidance and/or collaboration with more capable peers.
—Morgan and Saxton (1989, n.p.)

A Seminar Reflection
I find that I remember far more from classes that have a discussion component . . .
—Nicola Hart, 2002

conversations will occur; these are natural and an important means of scaffolding as students construct their understanding by building on peer and teacher input.

3 In this kind of discourse, the rhythm of the dialogue is similar to the rhythm of the students' own peer talk. This talk "rests upon a general consensus of opinion and attitude, yet individual differences are expressed. It is exploratory . . . it penetrates deeper . . . than a more structured, more objective analysis could have taken them" (Bruner, 1970, p. 243). When thought and feeling are focused and given expression, they cannot always be stopped by the ringing of a bell or a change of environment. Productive discourse can have a spill-over effect in which the participants continue the conversation outside the classroom, with you, other teachers, parents, and friends.

In enabling discourse, consider these factors:

1 The arrangement of the classroom plays a significant part in the success of the discourse. It should enable everyone to be in a position to read the non-verbal signals in conjunction with what is being said.
2 Your own personal intentionalities (which include your biases, attitudes, and values) should be used constructively and openly as part of the development of the discourse.
3 Your role will change from a position as the holder of knowledge and only controller of its revelations to that of a facilitator of learning: one who has a place, but not a central place, in the dialogue.
4 Finally, you must recognize that, because students have permission to talk, some ideas and attitudes expressed will conflict with and trespass on others' concepts and feelings (and, sometimes or often, upon your own). Northrop Frye (1988, p.184) warns that "as long as we have the words to formulate ideas with, those ideas will still be potential, and potentially dangerous." Effective discourse has its own built-in discipline. The individual feels a sense of responsibility to the group, the group feels a sense of responsibility to the individual, and there is a common commitment to the task.

Just as we have looked at the characteristics of effective classroom discourse, let us now examine the characteristics of effective questioning. To illustrate this, both in this chapter and later on, we will take a source that was used with general students, aged 16/17. The teacher's focus, to strive against great odds and not win the prize, was chosen because it matched the students' experience. Sometimes it is more effective to illustrate a point with a negative example—and we let you know when we are doing so, although we are sure you can see that for yourself.

Captain Robert Scott and his party of five left base camp in Antarctica in October 1911, with motor sledges, ponies and dogs, in their bid to be the first at the South Pole. The motors soon broke down, the ponies, unable to cope with the extreme cold, were shot and the dogs sent back to base because Scott was not prepared to sacrifice them. The polar party, themselves pulling the sleds, arrived at the Pole in January 1912, to find that they had been forestalled by the Norwegian explorer, Roald Amundsen. The weather on the return journey was exceptionally bad. Evans, the group doctor, died and Captain Oates sacrificed himself by walking out into a blizzard while his companions slept. The three survivors struggled on, but were confined at their next camp for nine days by the blizzard. All perished. Their frozen bodies were found by search parties in November 1912.

Characteristics of a good question

A good question is an expressive demonstration of a genuine curiosity; behind every question there must be the intention to know.

> I wonder what drives men to risk their lives in such adventures?

This question is rich with possibilities for issues of gender difference that the students leapt upon with delight; engagement was not a problem here.

A good question has an inner logic related in some way to the teacher's focus and the students' experiences.

> When Scott saw the Norwegian flag at the South Pole, what might have been in his mind? in the minds of his men?

In a good question, the words are ordered in such a way that the thinking is clarified both for the students and the teacher.

> Are you in favor of his not going at all, or his not taking dogs to the Pole?

What is the real question here?

> What would their chances have been had they kept the dogs instead of pulling the sleds themselves? *Or*
> Should someone who leads a perilous expedition allow his personal biases to endanger the lives of others?

The original question is a fine example of the *ambiguous* question.

In a good question the intent must be supported by intonation and non-verbal signals. The pace of the question should match the intent. Consider these alternatives:

> Teacher (*bright and sparkling, speaking quickly*): I wonder why Captain Oates would do a thing like that? *Or*
> Teacher (*speaking slowly and almost to herself*): I wonder . . . why Captain Oates . . . would do a thing like that?

Can you hear the difference?

A good question can provide surprise. Students will sometimes respond to a good question by talking about things that neither they nor the teacher was aware that they knew:

> Have you ever, at any time, risked someone else's life?

Students were amazed to discover how often they had, unwittingly, done just this. Although it did not directly fit the teacher's focus, an important discussion developed on the morality of responsibility and the fear of being thought a coward.

The essence of the question, said Gadamer (1975), is the opening up, and keeping open, of possibilities (266). But we can only do this if we can keep ourselves open in such a way that in this abiding concern of our questioning we find ourselves deeply interested (inter-esse, to be or stand in the midst of something) in that place which makes the question possible in the first place.
—Max van Manen (1992, p. 43)

A good question challenges existing thinking and encourages reflection:

> What makes a hero?

Students began defining a hero by referring to film actors. A stimulating conversation followed about whether someone who creates the *illusion* of heroism can be called a hero.

A good question is seen as part of an ongoing dialogue which involves relationships between speakers:

> John has just suggested they should have used cell phones. What might be the problem with that suggestion?

In public discourse, overt correction can shut down a student's contributions. Here, the teacher is correcting through the discourse. After a short discussion about the effects of cold temperatures on technological equipment, students realized the anachronism.

A good question has reason, focus, clarity, and appropriate intonation. It can challenge and surprise, but should not be seen as a weapon by which to diminish others. A good question maintains student engagement, stimulates thought, and evokes feelings. Discourse, however, is not just about the act of talking, of asking good questions; talk goes nowhere without a responsive listener.

Characteristics of an active responding process

The art of questioning involves not only the ability to make and deliver good questions; it also depends on the quality of the responding process. The three interdependent components of this process are (1) listening, (2) thinking, and (3) hearing one's own answer. The key to good questioning is *quality*, not quantity. Effective questioning demands active listening, thoughtful answers, and, of equal importance, time to think out a response. The characteristics of these components as they apply to the classroom are outlined below.

Active listeners
- are genuinely interested in the reply and willing to let it change them in some way (Laidlaw, 1989)
- are prepared to wait for answers
- are as interested in the responses of others as they are in their own
- are in tune with the social context of the classroom as well as the subject content

Quality thinking time
- depends upon everyone being comfortable with silence
- depends upon everyone being *seen* to be comfortable with silence
- is filled with the energy of curiosity balanced by the energy of thinking and feeling. Active silence speaks as loudly as words—an interrupted silence is equal to interrupting a speaker; thought is part of verbal expression and exchange.

If we take the assembly of language [seriously, as we should] do not expect instant answers. Developing a plan takes time—a few seconds at the very least and probably several minutes in many cases. But it is worth the time. Good questions take time, and so do good answers.
—James E. Zull (2002, p. 200)

Thoughtful answers
- can move the exploration on to a new stage
- can raise the exploration to a higher intellectual and emotional level
- show respect for the question
- may not come easily, but be marked with hesitancy and rephrasing (Barnes, 1976)
- reveal the level of thought and feeling in the responder
- often appear in the form of a question
- depend upon the care with which the questions were put

Why do teachers ask so many questions?

If statistics are to be believed—and we can see no reason for not believing them as they confirm our own experience!—teachers ask far too many questions. On an average day, some ask between 300 and 400 questions. When you eliminate the times when students are busy at other things, for example, deskwork, reading, recess, physical education, and eating, it would appear that teachers are asking a question every 5.6 to 11.0 seconds (Primary English Notes, n.d.).

Why do we do this?

- Is it because we believe that the more questions we ask, the more possibilities there are for learning?
- Is it because our view of ourselves as professionals endows us with the right and responsibility to ask questions and our view of students grants them the right and responsibility to give answers?
- Is it because we like talking more than listening?
- Is it because we have read that a good teacher asks questions, so we assume that by asking a lot of questions we will be better than just "good"?
- Is it because, as Benjamen (1981, p. 71) suggests, our questions seem to keep us "afloat" and if we took them away, we might sink?
- Is it because we use our questions to ensure that students understand that "we are the authority, the expert and that only we know what is important and relevant for them" (Benjamen, p. 72)?
- Is it because we use our questions to check attention, assess rote learning, test knowledge, control topics of discussion, and direct students' thought and action (Edwards and Mercer, 1987)?
- Is it because the more questions we ask, the more hope we think we have for coming up with a good one?

There is a lot of truth in these leading questions. Learning, as we have said, occurs as the result of questions. Questions serve to focus the objectives of the curriculum. A good teacher *is* a good questioner and statistics suggest that, for many teachers, questioning is indeed the central technique; however, a teacher is not a vacuum cleaner salesperson who is told that the more calls made, the more likely a sale. Although we might argue that the question is a house call on the mind, the analogy must stop there! Questioning is far too important to rely on the scattergun approach;

The Inquisitors were the first to formalize the idea that to every question there is a right answer. The answer is known, but the question must be asked and correctly answered. . . .
Questioning could, of course, be carried out without the crutch of torture. On the other hand, torture ensured an answer.
—John Ralston Saul (1993, pp. 41, 282)

it is also far too valuable a technique not to know what you are about when you are using it.

The art of questioning involves not only the ability to make and deliver good questions; as suggested above, it also involves answering. Where in this fusillade of questions is there room for an answer? Where is the time for students to think about answers, to choose the words to frame the answers and to speak the answers or to frame and articulate their questions? Where is the time for the teacher to consider the answers and to formulate a response to those answers? We use these questions as examples of a rhetorical device that will move us into the next section.

Thinking time

Thinking and feeling are internal activities that take energy and need time. *Wait time* is a term which refers to what the teacher is doing after she has asked a question. In a classroom built upon the principles of active participation, though, our term, *thinking time*, seems to more properly describe what is happening.

In the theatre, there are many words to indicate what is happening to the actor when the action is stilled: *pause, silence, waits, listens, thinks, holds, looks, stops*. These words do not mean that the internal (or dramatic) action has stopped, but rather that the expressive activity has stopped in order for the audience to become more aware of what is going on in the minds and hearts of the characters. These silences are filled with the actions of thoughts and feelings. So, too, the classroom when silence occurs.

Thinking and feeling are internal activities that take energy and need time. Today, pagers, cell phones, and personal communication devices demand immediate responses and, often, we feel a pressure to be in instant communication 24/7. As a result, many of our students can be really uncomfortable with silence—they have no idea what they are supposed to be "doing." It is important for teachers to help their students take time (or, rather, step out of time) and to understand how to make use of that new space.

The teacher's ability to wait calmly while students consider the question and formulate the answer

- builds trust in the relationship between teacher and students;
- gives time for students to look at the question from many angles;
- frees students to provide answers of substance;
- presses them to respond by speaking what is on and in their minds;
- suggests that they share the responsibility for their learning; and
- increases student-to-student interaction and student-to-teacher responses.

How long should you wait?

A faculty of education student handout states that teachers should "allow a pause time after you ask a question (3 seconds at least)." How long is three seconds? Not long, is it? Would you be surprised to learn

Quick answers are not necessarily the best. It is important to establish an atmosphere where you are seen to be prepared to wait.

Our current system, just telling kids to study, study, study, has been a failure. . . . telling them to study more will no longer work. . . . We want to give some time to think.
—Ken Terawaki, Japanese Ministry of Education (In Holt, 2002, p. 271)

Renowned literary theorist Northrop Frye was known for the long pauses in his lectures as he awaited questions from the class. A portrait by Jeff Sprang, one of his former students, shows the "ever-thinking" Frye in front of a blackboard, his hand on his chin, waiting—and thinking.
—Lisa Rundle (2005, p. 17)

that it is *two seconds longer* than most teachers wait for a response to their questions?

There are many statistics on the timing of what is called *question recitation* (see page 71). If we take a generous view of these statistics, we can assume that one question is asked every 10 seconds. It is expected that the teacher asks the question; the students think and formulate a reply; one student speaks the answer; and the teacher absorbs, considers, and weaves the answer back into the lesson context and focus all in a time frame of 10 seconds.

This timing means that the question will have to be short, direct, and simple, requiring an answer which is also short, direct, and uncomplicated by complex thought or feeling, resulting in a communication which is immediately applicable to the teacher's lesson plan. If they don't get instant answers, teachers tend to repeat or rephrase their questions, change their questions, or ask another student; then, as soon as a student makes a response, teachers tend to react immediately with praise, a new question, or some other interjection (Purkey, 1978).

Why is it so hard to wait?

The nature of social discourse lacks silence and in any conversational lull we remember the old social dictum: to keep the conversational ball rolling. We are not used to productive and constructive silence within everyday talk, "dead air" on the radio makes us anxious and unless the set breaks down, there is always something "going on" on TV. Our natural reaction in the classroom when a silence falls is discomfort and, sometimes, fear: fear that we have asked a poor question, that the students don't know the answer, or that the silence will act as an invitation for the students to fill it with something irrelevant, perhaps a smart-aleck remark.

When we do have the courage to increase thinking time, research demonstrates that significant changes occur:

• Students give longer answers.
• More students volunteer answers.
• More questions are asked by students.
• Student responses are more analytical, creative, and evaluative.
• Students report, "Class is more interesting" (Ferrara, 1981).

Isn't all this worth waiting for?

In Chapter 9, we suggest some techniques from which you can draw questions that will best serve your own particular classroom style.

Chapter 9 Putting the Question, Handling the Answer

In the previous chapter we talked about creating an atmosphere and environment for promoting effective questioning. We will begin here by looking at the general teaching requirements and techniques by which a teacher can help establish an environment in which questions and thoughtful answers become partners in a process of inquiry.

General teaching requirements

Classroom arrangement

Be aware of the arrangement of the classroom and your place in it. Staying at your desk with students arranged in rows facing you is not always appropriate for generating different kinds of discourse.

All students should be where they can see, hear, and make eye contact with one another. In this arrangement, participation is both encouraged and made easier.

You should be in a position to "catch" students' eyes because doing so is a way to invite response non-verbally. At the same time, it's important not to be "locked in." You need to be able to move around the classroom in order to step aside from a controlling position or to provide support by standing by a speaker.

Classroom conduct

Establish the rituals for "permission to speak." In some circumstances, you will need a raised hand; in others, particularly in free-flowing classroom discourse, it will be important to establish and reinforce the organic discipline of the talk—in these instances, formal permission to speak should not be required.

Establish, too, an atmosphere of general respect for the ideas and opinions of others. You can help to do this by modelling your attention and interest in your students' contributions.

Lesson focus and objectives

Recognize that the questions you have prepared may be inappropriate to the direction in which the discourse is moving; if so, restructure them in terms of the ongoing talk or else put them aside in order to pose questions that are more relevant. As long as you are clear about your *key* question(s) and your teaching objectives, restructuring or finding new questions to pose should not be a problem.

Observation

You need to be observant in order to pose questions that otherwise might not be considered, to pick up the *sotto voce* answer and the mood of the group, to be alert to unvoiced answers, and to be able to distinguish the smart-aleck answer from the answer based on a genuine misunderstanding. Ensure that in any dialogue (either between you and a student or between students) you find opportunities to throw the subject open to the whole group.

Voice and intonation

Be aware of the need for variety in the pattern of the discourse. People tend to pick up on the speech patterns of previous speakers. It is your responsibility to be conscious of this tendency and to ensure that the conversational drive maintains its impetus by stepping into the talk with a different rhythm and tone.

Be aware of how your intonations can change the meaning of what you are saying. It is not *what* words you say but *how* you say them which has the most significant personal impact. For example, consider this question:

> That is all the information you have found?

Depending on your intonation, it could mean any of the following:

(a) There isn't any more?
(b) The resource centre is even more inadequate than I thought!
(c) There is more and you've been too lazy to find it!
(d) Other people have been able to find more.
(e) Perhaps I gave you insufficient directions.

Try asking the example question aloud, using intentions (a) through (e), and hear the differences.

General teaching techniques

1. Use clear, direct language.

> Knowledge of the language of [a] subject . . . includes not only what its words mean but, far more important, *how* its words mean. As one learns the language of a subject, one is also learning what the subject is.
> —Neil Postman (1979, p. 149)

When asking a question, you need to use simple, clear direct language that allows students to connect with the thinking and the feeling behind the words. A question cloaked in complicated grammatical structure and high-sounding language rarely produces high-level, well-expressed thinking.

The words you use and the way in which you use them should put students inside the language of the material and of the subject so that the language they use in response will be appropriate to the content.

When a student joins you by answering, he is joining in the process of the inquiry with you. He wants to discover how to manipulate the language of the subject.

83

2. Elevate language.

Students can think in complexities, but they often use language poorly.

(a) They are simply careless, or the teacher has been careless in the ways she uses language.
(b) They lack the grammatical skills, a command of general vocabulary, or both.
(c) They do not possess the vocabulary of the subject discipline.
(d) They have experienced using language informationally, but lack experience in using it interactively and expressively.

Teachers, when engaged in discourse, have many opportunities to model a variety of language uses without being seen to be critical and correcting. For example, let's think about the text on Scott in Chapter 8:

> Teacher: In Norwegian history of Antarctic exploration, what reference might there be to Scott's expedition?
> Student: That he messed up!
> Teacher: Yes, it could be considered a failure by them.
> *Function:* To accept the idea and upgrade the language in a way that students can accept without taking offence

3. Give an answer weight.

Often in discourse a student will respond in a non-public way, as an aside, or respond unthinkingly. These remarks are sometimes very valuable and a listening teacher can pick them up and give them weight. For example:

> Student (*to another student sotto voce*): We certainly wasted a lot of time on a failure.
> Teacher (*smiling at the speaker*): Is it possible that we learn more through our failures than through being successful?
> *Function:* To see this casual and rather dismissive remark as a direct route to the focus of the lesson (without comment)

4. Universalize the answer.

Another way of responding to the casual remark above would be to help students see things in a wider context. The statement "There always have to be people who risk failure in order for progress to be assured" could be seen to reflect

(a) the wider context of history: Scott is one with all those throughout history who have tried and failed.
(b) the wider context of the need to be challenged: Scott is one with all those who are prepared to dare.
(c) the wider context of the competitive spirit: Scott is one with all those who want to be first.

5. Deal with a response which downgrades another's contribution.

There are a number of ways of dealing with this kind of remark:

> Student: Aw! That's stupid!
> Teacher:
> (a) So far, it's the only idea we have.
> *Function:* To give acknowledgment to the contribution, implying that others should try contributing
> (b) Perhaps, but do you have a better idea?
> *Function:* To remind students of the rules of brainstorming
> (c) Hold it! We're just brainstorming here!
> *Function:* A more overt reminder of brainstorming
> (d) Just a moment! Do we really understand what he said?
> *Function:* To show the class and the student who has made what was considered a stupid remark that the teacher is prepared to consider it
> (e) I am prepared to listen to all ideas.
> *Function:* To encourage the students to put forward more ideas

If a remark is truly offensive, it will be due to thoughtlessness, inattention, or the desire to disrupt. It should be dealt with accordingly and then the class should move on.

The Side Chat
An effective way to have students consider and reflect is to ask them to turn to the person beside them and talk. This technique provides opportunities to check in with someone else and try out some thoughts privately before offering them to the class and teacher.

6. Give opportunities for rethinking and restating.

> You still think that?
> You've changed your mind?
> *Function:* There are times when students need the opportunity to reconsider their original responses.

Or, you can take a more direct approach:

> What made you change your mind?
> How does that fit with what you were saying earlier?
> *Function:* In discourse students are often swayed by the views of others and it is important for them to be aware that they *have* changed their views and, more important, that they are able to describe what made them change. This type of question also helps the student to test out a new view of the situation or idea.

The next part of the chapter deals with specific questioning techniques.

Distribution, or targeting, of questions

Distribution, or *targeting*, refers to the way in which questions are directed.

(a) Questions can be directed at an individual, for example:

> John, what have you discovered that we need to know?
> *Function:* Here everyone but John can relax.

Another way of directing a question at an individual can generate a momentary tension for the class:

What have you discovered that we need to know . . . John?
Function: Here everyone is thinking and assessing, but can relax when John is given the responsibility for answering.

(b) Questions can be directed to a particular group:

What have you *boys* discovered that we need to know?
Function: The rest of the boys and all the girls can relax.

(c) Questions can be directed at the whole group:

What have you discovered that we need to know?
Function: Everyone is thinking and assessing and then may contribute.

There is nothing wrong with directing a question at an individual or a small group as long as you have a specific reason for so doing. Perhaps you are aware that John knows something of value from which all could benefit or you may have seen, as you asked the question, that John wants to answer it. It may be that you have noticed that John is nodding off and needs a wake-up call, or you may know that this particular group of boys needs one another's support as they answer.

Targeting has acquired a bad name. Apart from its unhappy associations with shooting, it is often used as a control—"You're fooling around; pay attention by contributing!"; as a means of showing up the lazy, the dull, or the "all-knowing"; or as a means of ensuring that everyone on the class list answers a question in turn. (We remember teachers who did the latter: it was most relaxing until they came to two names ahead of ours, at which time it was advisable to sit up and take notice!)

There are other problems with the ways in which teachers distribute questions:

- Some teachers tend to ask more questions of boys than girls (and vice versa).
- Some teachers give more questions to high achievers.
- Some teachers ask more questions of low achievers.
- Some teachers target specific kinds of questions to specific kinds of students: complex and abstract questions to the high academic students and simple, factual ones to the academically less able.
- Some teachers have a tendency to focus their questions to the right side of the class (or to the left); some work a fan shape; some work the triangle; some the front rows, some the middle, some the back rows. Students soon learn to gravitate to the hot spot if they want to be noticed and to the cold spots if they haven't done their homework, feel tired or bored, or need to complete an assignment for the next class.

Like the stand-up comic or club singer, you need to be aware of your own particular questioning distribution patterns in order to "work the room." The keys for unlocking general participation are to support the weak, encourage the students who are trying, tolerate (and see the potential for learning from) contrary opinions, and appreciate the contributions made by your most thoughtful students, as aids to your own teaching process.

Reinforcing for success

Other words for *reinforce*—fuel, brace (as in strengthen), succour, and nourish—point to the value of this technique. The effect of this technique is to give students a feeling of success, a feeling that they are on the right track which, in turn, gives them the sense that they have some control, some voice in directing their own learning. Reinforcement is a most effective way of encouraging participation. Different students respond to different kinds of reinforcement and there are many ways of supporting students and their work.

Verbal reinforcement

A Seminar Reflection
I realize that you can interest the student so much more if you become interested in the material. The inclusion of a simple "I wonder why . . ." can invoke intrigue and a sense of mystery from the question.
—Barton Hughes, 2002

Such words or phrases as "good," "well done," "that's interesting," and "good point" confirm for students that their contributions are not just accepted but approved.

Another means, probably the most powerful of all, is to use the students' words and ideas as part of your own teacher talk.

Student: Surely they could have found better ways of using their money than wasting it on badly planned exploration to a place no one is ever going to?

Teacher: I wonder how much money we've "wasted on badly planned" space explorations? (using the words) *Or*

Teacher: I wonder if we could say the same thing about our space explorations? (using the ideas)

Reinforcing is a powerful tool for encouraging participation but, if used dishonestly as praise for poor work, it loses its effectiveness. How then, can you acknowledge contributions that are sincere but off track or incomprehensible?

A word of warning: Don't fall into the habit of using reinforcing words or phrases as a means to fill in thinking time, either for yourself or while you are waiting for a response from someone else.

Here are some useful phrases to consider:

- Thanks for that answer.
- Remember our focus is. . . . Can we tackle this answer again, keeping that in mind?
- Yes, those ideas may be useful to us later on.
- Uh, huh. I hadn't thought of that.
- Yes. I'm not sure that we share enough of your reference points to take your meaning.

Minimal encouragements

These are audible prompts which indicate that either the teacher is interested in what is being said or that the student is to continue: "Hmmmm," "Ummmm," "Uh, huh," "So . . . ?" "Then . . . ?" "Yes . . . ?" "See. . . . " As with reinforcing comments, be careful not to rely on one or two prompts. They can become as irritating as those people who use "er" or "um"! Remember, too, that if silence is to be valued as a time to think, you need to be aware that your interjections are better used purposefully, but sparingly.

Non-verbal reinforcements

The earliest language was body language and, since this language is the language of questions, if we limit the questions, and if we only pay attention to or place value on spoken or written language, then we are ruling out a large area of human language.
—Paulo Freire and Antonio Faundez (Cited in O'Sullivan, 1998, p. 163)

The body itself is the most direct communicator of messages. *Non-verbal signalling* (also referred to as *body language*) can be a powerful means of both asking questions and reinforcing answers; it can also be a more direct and less threatening means of querying a contribution. You signal your involvement with your students by the way in which you make, hold, break, or lose eye contact; you signal your intellectual and emotional engagement by your facial expressions and body position.

Eye contact: Eyes have been described as the window of the soul. Eye contact is not about being eyeball to eyeball (which can be extremely threatening and inhibiting); it is about being able to see how students are connecting with you and how you are connecting with them. Girls are more comfortable with eye contact than boys, and respect in certain cultures is shown by the avoidance of eye contact.

Facial expression: We read reaction through facial expression: the raised eyebrow could mean, I don't understand; the frown could mean, This *is* interesting or What are you trying to tell me?; closed eyes could signify conspiracy, deep thought, or consideration; and the smile could suggest, You're doing well, keep going. There are, of course, negative reinforcements such as the curled lip, the flared nostril, the rolling eyes—all signals that what is being contributed is being received, judged, and found wanting!

Body gestures: Some examples of body gestures are nodding the head (That's right, keep going); shaking the head (Amazing! What will you think of next?); finger-pointing for emphasis, to isolate a place, or focus on a student; shaking the finger (Stop that! Let's get on); shrugging the shoulders (Who cares? Is that important?); giving the still look; and making a silent scan (Do you all agree with that? Are you ready?).

The silent language and the audible language must be congruent if they are to register the kind of reinforcement you intend.

Body positions: Where you stand or sit in relation to your students and when, how, and where you choose to move can be strong indications of your willingness to control or to hand over control. The shape of your body—leaning forward in your chair, leaning back against the wall—and what you are doing with your arms, hands, legs and feet—arms folded, twiddling fingers, swinging legs, tapping feet—all send significant signals that can promote and encourage, or inhibit and discourage engagement.

Eye contact, expression, gesture, and position are not actions that can be planned, but are your body's natural responses to your thinking and feeling. Non-verbal signalling is the primary message that your students read; therefore, it is imperative to be as aware of what you do and how you do it as of what you say and how you say it.

Probing for deeper thought

Probing is a technique designed to help students to think out answers more thoroughly, to encourage quantity and quality of participation, to require students to be more accurate and specific. Here are some useful probing questions: "Can you be more specific?" "What makes you think that?" "What about the other side?" "How might other people see this?"

A probing question can be used when a student has difficulty in finding the words to describe an abstract concept and so answers with concrete examples. The teacher can use concrete ideas as a base from which to build into the abstract.

> Teacher: What is nationalism?
> Student A: Flags.
> Student B: The national anthem.
> *Silence.*

The teacher hopes for more, but nothing more is forthcoming. At this point she needs to use "the probe":

> That could be an interesting way of looking at it. . . .
> *Function:* She is acknowledging and suggesting that there are other ways, but giving no help to find them.

But, alas, one is more likely to hear something like the following, included here so that you may recognize such responses in yourself:

> Come on. What else?

If they had known what else, the students would have said it.

> That isn't what I asked.

Nothing has changed except that by criticizing the teacher has probably closed down the discourse.

Had the teacher accepted the student responses of "flags" and "national anthem" and begun her probe at this concrete level, she might have been able to lead them into the abstract in this way:

> Teacher: Where have you seen a flag flying?

Student: Outside the school.

Teacher: How many of you notice the flag when you come into school in the morning? (*A show of student hands.*)

Teacher: I wonder why a national symbol flies over our school?

Student: To show that this is a Canadian school.

Teacher: Of what sorts of things does our flag remind us?

Student A: That we are all Canadians.

Student B: We are under the protection of Canada.

Student A: At the Calgary Olympics, it told the world that we were the host country.

Student C: When the Norwegians put up their flag at the South Pole, it told Scott who had got there first and who claimed the territory.

Function: Using the probe, the teacher is able to help her students state their ideas. From these they are able to arrive at a definition of nationalism.

The counselling probe

There are times when a student's personal experience influences his performance and a teacher will need to work with this student on an individual basis. We are not suggesting that the counselling probe replace the work of counsellors or psychologists, but teacher use of the technique may help the student reflect on a problem.

Student: Everyone in my group thinks I'm stupid.

Teacher: Who, specifically, thinks you're stupid?

Student: I know Mary does.

Teacher: How does Mary show that she thinks you're stupid?

Student: I just can't work with her.

Teacher: What stops you from working with her?

Student: She never listens to my ideas.

Teacher: Can you say, "I never listen to her ideas"?

And so on.

Using the probe in this way (reflecting the student's own words at an unhurried pace) can help him to look at an academic or personal problem. It is also a useful technique for analysing a group process and the student's part in it. In all cases, the teacher's stance must be one of non-judgmental *active* listening and her responses need to be "lean, concrete and relevant" (Roth, n.d.). The key words in the questions are Who? What? When? Where? and How? but *never* Why? The task is to help the student make meaning for himself and not to interrogate him.

When *not* to ask a question

It is possible that by now, you have decided that the only way to teach is through questions. There are, however, times when it is inappropriate to ask questions.

• Students have insufficient knowledge and experience from which to draw an answer: all students can do in this case is to share their ignorance, often reinforcing wrong information and allowing the expression of uninformed and ill-informed opinions. At this time, students should be encouraged to *ask* questions, not answer them.

- Students are working things out for themselves and making progress: you don't want to intrude on productive work however much you may know the right question to ask to put them into the solution! It is often a temptation to use a question as a means of entering a group discussion. "Are there any problems?" "How are you all getting along?" These are maddening interruptions that ask a group to move backwards into review just as they are moving ahead! It is better to sit on the fringe and listen. You will soon discover where they are and what difficulties they are having.

- We see a student who seems to be having problems: often, our first instinct is to ask a question because we naturally are concerned and perplexed. We have a terrible tendency to say something like, "Now, Chris, what seems to be the problem?" or "Are you all right?" It is much better to use a gentle statement such as, "You are very quiet today" and then become an active listener, allowing Chris to talk if he wants to talk about it. In this way he knows that you are aware and interested in him without demanding an answer which, possibly, he cannot articulate or which he may not want to articulate at the time.

Having taken these points into account, let us look at what happens after a good question has been asked.

Dealing with answers

The process of inquiry does not stop after the question is asked and the answer is given. Like a rally in a game of tennis, the ideas go back and forth for as long as they are able to be sustained. Being able to sustain the rally and send the ball back is as much a part of questioning technique as being able to put the ball across the net in the first place. The way in which you handle this part of the process will become a model for your students.

Let's examine one question-and-answer exchange and the kinds of responses it can generate.

> Teacher: Knowing the sort of hardship that would be experienced on the Scott expedition, what qualities would you look for in your team?
> Student: They would have to be strong.

The student's answer is perfectly acceptable and there are many ways of responding to it:

(a) By acknowledging the answer with a look or gesture and waiting
   Function: To indicate that the teacher is waiting for further suggestions
(b) By saying, "Ye . . . e . . . es"
   Function: Acknowledging the answer verbally and waiting for further answers
(c) By saying, "Yes, that is a useful quality."
   Function: Acknowledging and reinforcing the contribution, but remaining open for further suggestions

(d) By saying, "Yes, that's a useful physical quality."
    Function: Accepting the contribution but, by focusing on the physical, the teacher is suggesting that there are other aspects of quality
(e) By saying, "What kind of strength are you talking about?"
    Function: Accepting the contribution, but pressing the student to define what he means by the word "strong" in order to build common knowledge
(f) By saying, "What kind of strength is Glen talking about?"
    Function: Accepting Glen's idea as a stimulus for analysis by the class
(g) By saying, "Yes, you would have to be strong: physically, mentally and spiritually."
    Function: Accepting the student's words and idea and extending the concept because the teacher wants to move on quickly. It may be that Glen doesn't often contribute and she wants to make his contribution significant, or perhaps this class is not capable of seeing strength in anything other than physical terms and the teacher uses this opportunity to offer some abstract concepts.
(h) By saying, "If all our team is strong, will we need to look for experience?"
    Function: Accepting contribution, but pressing the class to look for implications: We can pull the sleds, but what if we don't know how to pack them?
(i) By saying, "Yes, the weak, the handicapped, the Stephen Hawkings of the world can never experience this kind of frontier exploration."
    Function: Accepting the idea and regretting the implications of it, thus allowing students opportunities to rethink

At times we hear an answer that we instinctively assess as superficial or perhaps typical of our class. Suppose the student answered the question "What qualities would you look for in your team?" by saying, "They'd all have to be rich." The teacher might react in a variety of ways:

All you kids think about is money.
I asked about *qualities.*
I suppose you'd be thrilled to have a rock star on your team.
Function: Here we can see that the teacher has heard only the word "money" which is the standard by which these students measure everything. She is reacting from her own emotional bias instead of hearing the truth of this reply: money *is* important in this kind of venture.

A better response:

Yes, these expeditions are expensive and the kinds of human qualities the team possesses will be very important if we don't want to waste the money.
Function: To accept what is given and elevate the thinking

The teacher can then either leave silence for students to think again about the question asked previously or decide to define what is meant by qualities. In working with Category B and C questions, such as the one under discussion here, it is difficult to have wrong answers, but there will be differences in the quality of the answers in terms of focus and language and intent. You will notice that when you deal with answers by responding to the ideas within the answer, you are following more closely the rules of normal conversation rather than evaluating the answer and asking another question as in recitation. For example:

> Good, Glen. Mary, what quality would you suggest? Okay, Nathan, what about you? Nathan, have you been listening? Pia, you usually have some interesting ideas . . .
> *And so on.*

Wrong answers and no answers

Susan Dressel (1981) did an interesting study in which she looked at student answers which appeared, to the teacher, to be wrong. Dressel discovered that, in many cases, the student's answer was right according to the reference base he was employing. In other words, we construct meaning out of the frames of reference we already have and when those don't relate to the teacher's, it can be extremely frustrating. She suggests that it is important for both teachers and students to "consciously discuss and identify their own and each other's reference bases" by asking a question like, "How do you know?" or saying, "Show me what you mean." Answers that appear to come out of nowhere or seem to be strange are coming from somewhere. A gentle "What makes you think that?" can be revealing and often useful.

If you are aware that your response has indicated to the student that his answer is either wrong or weak, you should try to return later with a question which will allow him to answer more positively, for example:

> Now that you have had time to listen to the others, what further ideas do you have about all this?
> *Function:* To provide the student with an opportunity to be successful and to let him know that one wrong answer does not exclude him from the conversation

Suppose you ask a question to which students cannot find an answer? It is important to let them understand that it is all right for them not to know. The responses "I don't know," "I don't know what you mean," "Could you say that another way?" or simply silence are not challenges to the teacher, indications of student stupidity, or evidence of teacher failure. They are valid responses by students (and even by teachers) and have their place in classroom discourse or discussion, just as they do in everyday conversation.

Any teacher response to a student answer will depend upon the class, the focus of the lesson activity, or the lesson and the kind of thinking and engagement the teacher wants or the students need. Acknowledgment, recognition, and the way in which you respond to student contributions are powerful means of generating classroom discourse.

Responding to answers: Some things to avoid

This section may appear to be repeating what has already been said but it demonstrates a number of common, but negative reactions that teachers

In other words, you might say that there is more to Knowing than just being correct.
—Benjamin Hoff (1982, p. 29)

make, often unintentionally and with the best interests of the students at heart.

1. Avoid manipulating responses by non-verbal signals.

Students are great sign readers and generally like to please. They can—and do—change answers in response to the signals you are sending

- by facial expressions: A frown can be read as "Do you know what you are saying?"; a smile can be read as "Not bad for a dumb kid!"
- by gestures: A finger snap can be read as "Hurry up!"; a dismissive turn of the head can be read as "I wish you weren't in my class."
- by non-verbal utterances: The sigh in "Yes, Kirk" can be read as "I never expect a right answer from you"; an in-drawn breath can be read as "What nonsense!"

These kinds of expressions have more power to discourage, antagonize, mock, and patronize than any words that you may choose to say. In reading these messages, students may adjust their answers (and their behavior) in order to restore their comfort level.

2. Avoid verbal responses that are detrimental to learning.

- Sarcasm: "Well, we do seem to know a lot about Scott, don't we?"
- Vague and ambiguous statements: "Oh, I suppose that answer is close enough."
- Leaping to *your* conclusion:

> Student: They should have eaten the dogs.
> Teacher: So you believe in vivisection?

3. Avoid responding with "Yes, but . . . " or "Yes, and . . . "

Inadvertently, you may put yourself back into a control position by responding to a student's contribution by using either of these constructions.

> Student: I think that if I'd been Scott's son, I would have resented that he threw away his life.
> Teacher: Yes, but surely you would have enjoyed being the son of a hero?
> *Or* Yes, and he might have lived to do other extraordinary deeds.

In both these replies the teacher has taken the initiative away from the students. In the "Yes, but" response, there is an unspoken criticism in the teacher's follow-up which, although a question, does not really invite an answer. In the "Yes, and" response, the teacher has taken over the student's idea by completing the thought herself. Much better to remember the lesson focus, acknowledge the answer, and wait to see if other students have anything to contribute.

4. Avoid reacting to every contribution.

Reacting to every student contribution with some kind of verbal response, such as "Good," "Right," or "Well done," refocuses the attention onto the teacher. It inhibits student-to-student interaction. Nothing can be more detrimental to discourse than to have students looking to the teacher for an evaluation of every response. Your attitude of interest and attention will be sufficient.

5. Avoid reinforcing prejudices.

> Student: If there'd been Black explorers, they wouldn't have got lost in the blizzard.
> *General laughter.*

Remarks such as this can offer opportunities for learning; however, teachers tend to over-react. Consider the effects of these alternatives:

> And what do you mean by that, Jeff?
> *Function:* Upgrading a remark that is not worthy of that kind of attention
> I won't have those remarks in my class. Go to the office!
> *Function:* The teacher is again giving more status to the remark than it deserves and letting the vice-principal deal with the situation.
> And you, Jeff, would easily be found in a dark jungle.
> *Function:* The teacher is playing Jeff's game, and by so doing is suggesting that jokes about color are acceptable.

Here are some positive ways of dealing with remarks of this sort:

> Jeff, whatever you mean by that, it's not worthy of you. Janet . . .
> *Function:* The teacher acknowledges that she has heard the remark and does not approve and moves on.
> *Or*
> Matthew Henson explored in the Arctic. It's only now that we are recognizing his contributions. He was Black. Janet . . .
> *Function:* The teacher defuses Jeff and diffuses the remark by giving out new and interesting information. She moves on.
> *Or*
> Janet, why do you think it took so long to find them?
> *Function:* The teacher ignores the remark and moves on, thereby implying that the remark was inappropriate and Jeff should know it.

6. Avoid asking questions to which students cannot possibly know the answer.

For example:

> What do you think I've got in store for you today? *Or*
> I wonder what I would have done if I'd been Captain Scott, Mary?
> *Function:* An example of what *never* to do

7. Avoid asking for choral answers.

Some elementary teachers are especially prone to prompting this kind of response.

> Captain Scott was a hero. All heroes are great men. Therefore, Captain Scott was a . . . [*altogether now*] . . . ?

Choral answers are a technique of rote learning, *not* what this book is about!

8. Avoid answering your own question!

What was the reaction in England when they heard of Scott's death? Naturally, they would have been very proud of his achievement . . . deeply sorry for his young family . . . disappointed that he wasn't first . . .

It takes a confident student to reply, "You've already answered your own question!" Nothing is more frustrating for a student than having a teacher do this just as he has come up with what he considers to be a really good answer.

9. Avoid counter-questioning.

Teachers think that students learn through questions. They do. These questions do not, however, need to be asked only by the teacher. When a student asks a question, try not to respond with one of your own.

Student: What kind of dogs did Scott take to the Pole?
Teacher: What breed do you think would suit those conditions?
Student: I don't know. (*He wants to add, "That's why I asked you."*)

Research has found that elementary teachers counter-question two of every three student questions (Dillon, 1983): "A counter-question says, 'I'm the one that asks the questions around here'" (p. 37). Rather than countering, the teacher could ask the rest of the class if anyone has the information or answer the question herself, if she knows or she could ask someone to find out the answer.

10. Avoid asking questions that have already been answered.

In the talk following the question "What preparations were made for the journey?" the students discussed at some length the kinds of food that would not spoil when frozen. The teacher then asked, "What kind of food did they carry with them?" What she is signalling is that she was not listening to the discussion, only waiting to ask the next question on her plan.

11. Avoid asking another question before the students have had time to contribute answers.

When you ask rapid-fire questions at your class, it promotes a pattern suggesting that questions can have only one, perhaps two answers.

Teacher: What kind of man was Oates?
Student: He was a romantic.
Teacher: Would you say that of his companions?

By the second question, 29 other possible contributions to the character of Captain Oates are lost.

12. Avoid redirecting a right-answer question.

Research demonstrates that this kind of redirection gives the impression to students that the first answer received was incorrect.

> Teacher: What is Scott's first name, Arthur?
> Arthur (*promptly*): Robert.
> Teacher: Mary . . . ?
> Mary: (*pause*) Well . . . [thinks, *I'm sure Art was right* . . .]
> Teacher: Joan. What was Scott's first name?
> Joan: [thinks, *Mary's usually right . . . she doesn't know . . .*] *She shrugs.*
> Teacher: Paul . . . ?
> Paul: (*looking up from doodling in his textbook*) Robert.

The teacher is hoping to see how many of her students know this information, but her students assume from past experience that the first answer was wrong and desperately look for the correct one. Paul is sure enough of himself and his knowledge to be bored by this foolish exploration.

13. Avoid collecting answers until you get the one you want.

> Teacher: What other events in modern times would be analogous with Scott's expedition?
> Student: The Canadian attempt on Everest?
> Teacher: Y . . . es.
> Student: People who try to get to the North Pole by motorcycle, or on skis, or whatever . . .
> Student: Carl Lewis . . . Steve Nash?
> Student: Lots of athletes don't come first.
> Student: Didn't the Russians try to get to the moon, too?
> Teacher (*enthusiastically*): Y . . . ES!
> Student: What about the *Challenger*?
> Teacher: RIGHT!

There are a lot of good answers here, any of which might have developed new perspectives on the teacher's focus; however, she was looking to her students to confirm her own thinking.

14. Avoid phrasing the question for the answer you want (a.k.a. the *leading* question)

For example:

> You wouldn't want to do that, would you?
> I don't think that would work, do you?
> Surely you don't think that?

Who would be foolish enough to disagree? Questions such as these *may* be used effectively with a soft and concerned tone and empathetic body language; otherwise, they are heard as "put downs" that discourage students and ensure their lack of engagement in further work.

15. Avoid hearing only what you want to hear.

Teachers must be careful not to hear only what they want to hear. Students will see the teacher as having a listening problem if what happens after they have contributed doesn't fit into the logic of their thinking and the dialogue. They may have thoughts like these:

This isn't the way she wants it to go.
What does she want?
Why can't she hear what I am not saying?
Why doesn't she just get on and teach us what she wants us to know and stop asking these questions?

Reactions like these can inhibit student contributions.

16. Avoid insincere praise.

Don't say, "Good try, Emily" when Emily has obviously not tried at all. Using praise as a means of "jollying" the students along when the quality of their work does not merit it destroys the questioning process. Undeserved praise will quickly put an end to any attempts at critical thinking, clarity, and accuracy. Students resent praise when they know they haven't earned it—it makes earned praise seem worthless. Reserve your praise until it is justified.

17. Avoid asking questions too soon.

Sometimes, students have been involved in an experience at a deeply personal level. Expecting them to talk about it before it has had time to settle will be unproductive. It can also destroy or trivialize the experience for them.

18. Avoid asking questions when students are too tired to think.

Despite the fact that nothing may seem to be happening, thinking is a very demanding activity. There will be times during the school year—after a football game or during the school play, for example—when your students are too tired to think and your questioning skills raise no response. It is more productive to put your students into some sort of physical task or ask them to put their heads down on their desks and listen to some music for 10 minutes. After that, they are usually ready to engage with the material.

In this chapter, we have looked at general teaching techniques that will help establish a nourishing environment for classroom inquiry. In the next chapter, we will look at why it is so important for students to be included as questioners in this process, examine the major impediments to their inclusion, and suggest ways of overcoming them.

Chapter 10   The Case for the Student as Questioner

No one would deny that we learn more in the first three years of our lives than in any other similar time period. The process of inquiry starts from the moment of birth and the acquisition of language is the result of that process and, at the same time, the tool for that process. Small children, as we know, are the most persistent of questioners:

What are you doing?
Planting seeds.
What are seeds?
They grow into flowers.
How?
Rain and the sun help.
Does the rain make me grow? . . .
And so on until the parent says, finally and firmly,
Because.

At home before attending school, children see themselves as "partners in dialogue" with their parents. Research demonstrates that they initiate *more than half* of the questions asked (Edwards and Westgate, 1987, p. 170). They are learning through questions: theirs and those of others with whom they come in contact. If children do learn through questioning and the purpose of schools is to further learning, it would seem logical that the ratio of approximately one adult question to one child question would be maintained throughout the child's schooling.

In a time of two-parent families where both parents may work outside the home and of single parent families, opportunities for conversational partnerships for the young child seem to be greatly reduced. One might expect preschool experiences to fill the gap left by family structure; however, most homes still provide better opportunities than the schools for learning through talk with an adult. In the Tizard and Hughes investigation (1984), children asking more than 50 percent of questions at home were asking *under 5 percent* of them in their nursery schools! Research shows little increase in students taking responsibility for questioning in their schooling, and a multidisciplinary study, *Questions and Discussion* (Dillon et al., 1988a), revealed that, in the senior grades, students were still asking less than 15 percent of the questions. A visit to a high school classroom today will confirm that the situation remains much as Windschitl (2002) describes in the next featured quotation.

Why aren't more questions coming from students?

If questioning is a powerful way to learn as well as to teach, why are there not more questions coming from students? There seem to be six main reasons, all of them pressures on classroom teachers:

- personal pressure—The teacher wants to be seen as "in control."
- right-answer pressure—Parents and school administrators put pressure on teachers to demonstrate that students possess the knowledge to enable them to gain high marks.
- curriculum pressure—Teachers are under pressure to cover an ever-growing curriculum.
- classroom environment pressure—conventional classroom arrangements appear to require that teachers conform to traditional teaching methods.
- control pressure—The teacher wants to be seen by colleagues, administrators, and the students as in control of herself, her students, and her subject.
- standardized testing pressure—The standards that must be achieved by students in external examinations, or "high stakes testing," place pressure upon teachers.

These are six realities and we are not so out of touch with reality as to suggest that teachers ignore parents and administration, forget about exams, throw out the curricula, risk dismissal, and make life miserable for themselves, their students, and their colleagues. But even taking all these pressures into consideration, if we accept that children are natural questioners and that they learn by questioning—and if we are in the business of learning—then it would seem imperative that we make room in our teaching for our students to capitalize on their natural ability to question.

In a study of schools undergoing reform, it was found that most teachers, administrators, and parents expected a . . . classroom to be quiet and orderly, with students seated and not talking to each other. Engagement meant that students were attentive but without speaking, gesturing, building things, or moving about.
—Mark Windshitl (2002, p. 150)

Addressing the pressures against the teaching of questioning skills

A study by Good et al. (1987) indicates that if the environment is appropriate and the adults in the environment are open, knowledgeable, and supportive, those systemic conditions mentioned above can be overcome. We offer some suggestions and comments.

Personal pressure

For teachers and especially teachers new to the classroom, there is the fear that we may not know the answer to a student's question. But what does this say about how we view the role of teachers in general and ourselves in particular? You want your students to see you as a learner, too. If you do not know an answer, it is a fine opportunity for them to help you and, in the process, discover a little about becoming a researcher. There is no reason for you not to say: "Haven't a clue, but I will try and find out. Don't forget to ask me about that next class"—and remember to make a note of it and find out!

Often, student questions can make us uncomfortable, so it is important to set guidelines about what is or is not appropriate. We have a colleague who teaches public speaking. He makes it very clear from the outset that religion, politics, and sex are topics that will not be addressed. When his students question him on this, he asks them why they are not considered suitable topics for dinner table conversations. The discussion that follows often reveals other topics that make people uncomfortable and that they would prefer not to be used.

Sometimes, we are concerned that we will be losing control of our teaching (not necessarily of the students) when students raise questions that are "beside the point" of the curriculum material. What are the implications of ignoring things simply because they appear to be "beside the point"? It is sometimes useful to ask the student, "Help us to see how what you are saying is relevant to what we are learning." You may be surprised at what you hear and find it a valuable inquiry. Of course, good questions lead to good talk and good talk happens when people care about something. That kind of talk can be noisy (oh, oh!), it can take time to sort out ideas, and you don't want to be seen to be wasting time.

Finally, it simply does not occur to some of us to invite students to ask questions. Howard Gardner, in *The Unschooled Mind* (1991), writes about the power of early learning and how easy it is for us when we become teachers, to fall back into old patterns of classroom behaviors that mirror our own experiences. If we were not invited to ask questions, it is easy for us to forget to do so with our own students.

Right-answer pressure

Tests and exams deal mainly with objective knowledge, known facts, and information. Therefore, the questions that are asked are ones to which there are, most often, right answers. Egan (1987) goes so far as to suggest that the test questions examine only the "most superficial" level of understanding. If a teacher teaches only to this agenda, there is no place for the kinds of questions that stimulate a variety of possible answers and generate thoughtful questions in return. Let's look at how two teachers might handle this matter. In a unit on environmental studies, the following were test questions:

1 Describe the qualities of Freon gas.
2 What is the effect of Freon gas on the ozone layer?
3 How important is the ozone layer to world environments?

Teacher A teaches the definitions of Freon gas and the ozone layer and describes the importance of the ozone layer. The right answers to the test questions demonstrate the effectiveness of her teaching of the facts and the students' ability to listen, store, and retrieve the facts.

Teacher B assigns reading on the material and asks the class to consider, while they are reading, something the teacher overheard in the supermarket: "After suffering through last winter, the world can't warm up too soon for me!" Class time is given over to discussion on this statement, during which the teacher's focus is to ensure that the test questions cited above can be answered. Her role in the discussion group is to offer support, opposition, alternatives, and information as the need arises.

The pursuit of greater objectivity in the name of greater accountability has resulted in an increase in the number of formal classroom evaluations—perhaps in the misguided belief that averaging a large number of somewhat subjective assessments delivers a more objective mean.
—Heather-Jane Robertson (1998, p. 65)

In school, a student's job is to get the right answers; in apprenticeship, a learner's job is to find, ask, answer and outgrow the right questions.
—Eric Booth (1999, p. 260)

Teacher A will know from test results that the students know (or do not know) what they need to know. Teacher B will know from the discussion that students know (or do not know) the answers to the three questions. She will know, as well, more about what her students think and feel about that knowledge.

Teacher A asks three questions and her students none.

Teacher B makes a declarative statement and most of the questions that follow come from the students during discussion and, in the main, are asked of one another.

Teacher A spends 30 minutes teaching to the above test questions.

Teacher B spends 30 minutes learning what her students know (some of which is not in the assigned reading), learning about her students and, incidentally, learning what her students know and she does not.

We are not suggesting that Teacher A is an incompetent teacher or that it is unimportant to know when to teach this way. What we are suggesting is that there are other ways of evaluating what students are learning and that it is more likely that they will retain that which they have found out for themselves.

Curriculum pressure

Where knowledge is cumulative teachers feel a responsibility to colleagues to make sure that students are equipped with the prerequisite information when they move on to the next grade level. With this kind of responsibility, teachers feel that they cannot "waste time" with activities that appear to be peripheral to the content.

If you consider that schools at best cover only a fraction of human knowledge and experience, then you will have to ask what content your students cannot do without.

Curriculum guides make the first selection by offering a survey of the material from which teachers can develop their individual courses of study. The next selector is you, the classroom teacher: you decide in discussion with your colleagues on which areas you will focus. For example, will you and your students explore medieval history through its wars? its economic development? its religious conflicts? Or, will you see the medieval world through the eyes of a small village? You make your choice on the basis of your personal preferences and upon your students' frames of reference. Whatever choice you make will, of course, include all aspects of the area of study (economy, conflicts, social organization and so on), as they affect your focus. Can you see, then, how the following questions for discussion need not be peripheral to the content?

1 Who might we consider as modern-day crusaders?
2 I don't suppose our societal structures are any less hierarchical than they were in feudal times?
3 Under what circumstances would a community today feel the need to isolate itself?

How you teach is entirely dependent upon your answer to the question *What is it you want your students to learn?* If your answer is that students must become manipulators and questioners, as well as receivers of knowledge, it will be possible for you to find opportunities for students

---

Stewart and Brendfur (2005, p. 685) write that "determining right and wrong answers [is] not the goal. Instead it [is] the thinking, reflection, and dialogue . . . that [becomes] important."

Insufficient time to teach basic subjects, introduction of new subjects, and tighter school budgets are some of the factors creating crowded curricula.
—*Arts Education Research Agenda for the Future* (1994, p. 9)

to question within your course time allocations. As one teacher put it, "We should be in the business of helping our students to *uncover*, not to cover, the curriculum."

Classroom environment pressure

Rows of desks facing the blackboard, the isolation of the teacher from the group, and the inflexibility of the furniture do not encourage easy classroom interaction and the authority of the curatorial staff inhibits most teachers from creative interior design! The time and the physical strain required to rearrange a classroom and then to restore it to its traditional arrangement can be seen as hardly justifying the possible learning outcomes.

First-year teachers who don't feel that they can "make demands" suffer from this constraint especially. If you can't move the desks, though, you can move the students: they can turn around and talk to the person behind; they can talk to the person across the aisle; they can sit on their desks to form small conversation groups.

You can arrange to move the class to a more flexible space such as the resource centre or the cafeteria, where the tables lend themselves to group discussion; some music and drama rooms offer carpeted floors which facilitate changing group sizes. From our experience, it is more satisfactory if you can manage in your own classroom; there is a sense of home, of security that is psychologically very supportive to classroom discourse. If you have movable furniture, you can redesign the room (after consultation with other colleagues who may be using the room and the curatorial staff) or you can train your students to shift the furniture and put it back with minimum confusion.

A changed environment is a learning motivator: it presents opportunities for those students whose learning styles do not fit the traditional classroom model; it changes the position and the status of the teacher, enabling changes in class empowerment; it promotes a different kind of talk and opportunities for peer learning and teaching. Students more readily engage in question-and-answer exchanges with one another than with their teachers and "students' responses to fellow students are longer and more complex than responses to the teacher" (Dillon, 1988b, p. 154). All of which, we believe, more than justifies finding the ways and the means.

Control pressure

A classroom full of student talk is often viewed with the suspicion that the teacher is a poor disciplinarian because, to the outsider, the class appears to be out of control. This perception is a major problem because it attacks the very foundations of what is teaching and what is a teacher. When the students are talking, the teacher is seen to be *not* in control, to be *not* teaching, the implication being that she isn't earning her money.

Students support this control pressure in two ways. Students who are used to authoritarian teachers who control the subject and ways students think about that subject, often respond in an aggressive or resentful manner when offered empowerment: they feel insecure with the changed rules. On the other hand, if the students are enjoying their participation

In *How the Mind Works*, Steven Pinker writes about the "kinds of places that human beings enjoy being in." He includes "cozy spaces" that give a sense of refuge, "a view with prospects," and a "sense of mystery" that hints of things to be discovered. These "environmental aesthetics" could serve as a metaphor for an effective classroom (1997, pp. 375–378).

The obsession with coverage leads to bored students who are rarely engaged in their own learning. Because teachers assume the responsibility of being the "worker" in the classroom, students have little responsibility in the teaching/learning process.
—William Patterson (2003, p. 570)

and expressing their enjoyment to others, then the course may be seen by other students and teachers as "mickey mouse," where everyone does what they want. Again, by implication, the teacher is not controlling either students or subject.

Students at all grade levels want the assurance that school is a place for answers because their outside world is so full of questions that don't appear to have answers. They want to see adults as people who can control things. When the teacher asks questions to which she does not know the answers, some students may go home and say, "Our teacher is stupid; we had to tell her everything!" That kind of perception tends to reassure neither parents nor students about the teacher's competency!

Standardized testing pressure

The need for external examinations is the result of political will. The purpose of these examinations is to discover what students have been taught. In a globalized world, the educational competition stakes are not just a matter of knowledge acquisition, but of national pride and possibly even economic necessity. In the interests of collecting results and comparing data, external examinations have been rationalized or standardized. Standardization relies upon materials that are designed by someone other than those for whom the examinations are intended; they do not take into account cultural differences, instructional and community values, teacher and student interest and needs. The result is that the curriculum is narrowed, tests come to define our priorities, and certain subjects and answers are privileged over others.

There has been a growing unease among teachers who feel the results [of standardized testing] don't account for the socio-economic factors that contribute to test scores.
—Gary Mason (2006, p. S1)

External examination questions differ from the kinds of questions we have been suggesting. They have to be carefully considered so that the answers can become part of a marking scheme that is as equitable for the student in Vanderhoof as it is for the student in Vancouver. The thrust then, is towards those questions that are fact- and information-based. Where these questions invite opinion, it would be unwise of a student to offer creative and critical-thinking answers unless he was confident that they matched accepted thought. The answer to the question "What forces shaped the character of Hamlet?" would not be the time for him to adopt the thesis that Hamlet was homosexual, however well he is able to support that argument.

While there are no hard data yet, it appears that schools may be doing more grouping and tracking in order to maximize the efficiency of test preparation.
—Alfie Kohn (2004, p. 575)

There are many other reasons for outside examinations: institutions of higher education want an objective yardstick to measure their intake; parents and students want high marks which will guarantee entrance to the next level of education. Test results provide the kind of information that parents are looking for when shopping for a suitable school for their children; administrators, too, are interested in the reputation of their schools. Buried in all these reasons are classroom teachers who are aware that they, too, are being examined and are concerned that students' poor results may affect their positions.

Outside examinations have been with us for a very long time. We remember the practice of streaming children who were seen as poor learners into technical or (in our case) home economics classes that did not have outside examinations. One colleague remembers his classroom seating plan changed in the spring of a "test" year: those students who

Suggestion for Reflection
Present students with the area of the subject to be studied. Ask them to write down what they already know about it; what questions they might have about it; and how they think it might be useful to them now or later. Put their responses in an envelope to be returned for reflection at the end of the unit.

were doing well sat in the rows next to the window, students who had little hope of passing sat near the door, and students who needed more attention were seated in the middle rows. In that way, the teacher could concentrate on those students and leave the others to get on (or not) by themselves.

It seems to us that it is only realistic to accept that standardized testing is not going to go away. We need to consider not only how we deal with it but how we can help our students to continue to learn. One of the most useful ways to deal with these situations is to ensure that your students understand that you are teaching "to the test" and that it is important for them to use this opportunity for learning. Once that is clear, everyone is better able to get on with what has to be done. Some students enjoy the challenge of the competition with its clearly defined parameters. Students who have learned how to learn and are familiar with cooperative inquiry and classroom discourse seem better able to cope successfully with external exams than those who have experienced only traditional classroom methodology. It is our experience that the former tend to be more adaptable and flexible in their approaches to tasks, whatever they may be.

Although we know that standardized testing has little to do with education as we would like it to be, it does relate to training and practice. If presented to students as a challenge, they can see some of the values of working to the test.

Teaching in ways that promote responsibility for learning

Despite the many pressures that teachers face, there is an even more compelling need to teach in ways that ask students to take more responsibility for their learning. Only by addressing that need can we be assured that our children will become effective citizens in the democracy. With this in mind, here are some suggestions that may help you to deal with the concerns that are raised about the use of inquiry-based or constructivist classrooms.

- You will need to know why you are teaching in this way and that you have sufficient ways to assess the learning outcomes. It will take time to find the techniques that work for you and your students.
- You have to understand that your students also need time to adjust to a more demanding learning process: they need time to develop the skills of discourse, to develop confidence in their abilities to work in this way, and to perceive that this is an interesting way to learn. It is often a long process until you arrive at the point where your students are ready to accept that, without their contributions, the work cannot proceed. Establishing the criteria for a new kind of teaching/learning process is a time of risk for both teacher and students so the signals have to be clear and the agenda open. Once established, however, a new classroom relationship will develop.
- You will discover that when students are engaged by the content and taking responsibility for their own work, discipline and management problems are minor and the students themselves often resolve the problems that do occur.

- Colleagues who are interested in how children learn will be supportive; however, you must accept that those who teach to a different agenda will probably continue to question your methods.
- You will need to take time to talk to your principals and head teachers about the kind of teaching and learning that you are practising, so that they will know what to look for when they come into (or pass by) your classroom. You will find, as we have, that they are enthusiastic and helpful. Remember, they and their administrators are being made aware daily, through conferences, memos, the media, and their political bosses, of the sorts of persons and the kinds of skills that are required in the 21st century.
- Consider a team approach, working with colleagues and administrators to research alternative ways of assessing students' annual yearly progress so that multiple indicators of school performance can demonstrate students' achievements over the year more inclusively. (See Kim and Sunderman, 2005.)
- Part of the maturation process is accepting that adults can be wrong, that there are answers but everyone may not know them, and that there are some questions for which we have not yet found the answers. The significant part of your job as a teacher is to offer students the means by which they can take control of their lives: to equip them to find the questions that will provide the answers—*for* themselves and by themselves. You will also want to make sure that your students understand that this is the purpose of their education.

If we accept that and believe students learn through their own questions, then we will have to provide more opportunities than we presently do for them to participate as questioners.

Although children are natural questioners, their talents are not necessarily going to develop without assistance. Consider that the musically gifted, the "natural" writer, the well-coordinated athlete all thrive in a supportive environment, exposure to the best in the field, training by enlightened teachers, and many opportunities to practise.

In the next chapter we will examine how you can model "relevant, appropriate and substantial questions," deliberately design lessons where students can learn about this "neglected language art" (Postman and Weingartner, 1969), and ensure that there are many opportunities for your students to switch places with you to practise their questioning skills.

I expect very little resistance to the claim that in the development of intelligence, nothing can be more "basic" than learning how to ask productive questions.
—Neil Postman (1979, p. 140)

Chapter 11 Switching Places: The Student as Questioner

If we respect students' abilities to define their own experiences, to generate their own hypotheses, and to discover new ways of categorizing the world, we might not be so quick to evaluate the adequacy of their answers. We might, instead, begin listening to their questions. Out of the questions of students come some of the most creative ideas and discoveries.
—Ellen Langer (1997, p. 135)

At present you need to live the question. Perhaps you will gradually, without even noticing it, find yourself experiencing the answer, some distant day.
—Rainer Maria Rilke (1875–1926)

In the last decade, there has been a great deal of encouragement for the development of "inquiry-based" or "problem-based" curricula. Examples of such curricula provide well-considered questions that the teacher asks and suggestions for generating student discussion. There is, however, little about helping students generate questions of substance that go beyond the informational. One of the first ways of providing that help is by becoming an exemplar yourself.

Modelling how to question

"Every time you ask a question you are presenting that question as a model to your students and modelling effective questions will help your students to ask better questions themselves" (Hunkins, 1974, p. 77). There are two ways in which you can model: covertly and overtly. By *covertly*, we mean that you hope your students will learn by osmosis; by *overtly*, we meant that you draw attention to what you are modelling by using a think-aloud or talk-about approach demonstrating to your students that you, too, need to consider how to phrase a question and that you appreciate, and are interested in, effective question-making.

The hallmarks of effective covert modelling are outlined here:

- Your questions will have reason, focus, and curiosity and in some way, they will hook in to the students' frames of reference.
- Your questions will be directed at uncovering information, building meaning, and considering implications.
- You will, by listening and thinking along with them, let your students experience the excitement and satisfaction that good questions stimulate.
- You will encourage *their* questions so that your students will come to understand that questions belong as much to them as to you.

Just as actual words are only a small part of how we hear, so, too, we should not underestimate the power of our covert modelling as a component in the teaching and learning process.

Overt ways to model questions

In looking at ways to increase student learning, Drake (1998) explores a number of models of integrated curricula in which question-asking by students is an important component. It became clear that "asking questions is a skill that improves with explicit instruction" and that further development of both the student and the subject was dependent upon being a "good questioner" (p. 146).

As a teacher, you have many opportunities to identify and model effective question making for your students. The statements and questions given below point to a variety of strategies that you can adopt. These include thinking aloud about questions, praising students' efforts, offering encouragement, and providing focus on the nature of questions.

Thinking aloud

Just a moment. I have to think how best I can put this question.
Function: Modelling that the arrangements of words are important in making an effective question

I need a little time to find the right question to open this up.
Function: Modelling that any old question does not do!

I know there is a question here, but I'm not sure what it is.
Function: Modelling that teachers not only don't have answers, but sometimes can't even find the question. This statement also offers an opportunity for the students to suggest a question.

Praising

That's a question that makes us think!
Function: Acknowledging a good question

I hadn't thought of that question.
Function: Acknowledging that good questions don't come only from the teacher

Hasn't this group's questions revealed some surprises?
Function: Acknowledging a group's effort to dig deeply into an idea

Encouraging

Your questions are getting better and better!
Function: Acknowledging students' developing skills as questioners

I've heard you ask better questions than that.
Function: Encouraging them to think more deeply and not to slip back

Today your questions made me think.
Function: Encouraging them to see that their questions are helping the teacher learn

Reflecting/Analysing

What was the question that got us going?
Function: Helping students to think critically about questions

Skillful inquiry includes seeking and trying good, and then better questions, as well as the ongoing answering.
—Eric Booth (1999, p. 100)

108

Why was that question so interesting to us?
Function: Analysing the qualities of a question

I wonder if there was another way we could have asked that question to get at a more detailed answer?
Function: Realizing that the form of a question controls the quality of the answer

Focusing

The questions we ask are going to be important, so we must make them carefully.
Function: Drawing attention to how the questions are made

As we are allowed only one question, what is it we need to know and how will we phrase the question to get that information?
Function: Pointing out that one question, well phrased, is better than 20 indifferent ones

Whenever your students are engaged in work that demands that they question one another, you as their teacher, or the subject, it offers an opportunity to reinforce that they are working effectively. If they are "sitting close together, watching the faces of people talking, asking questions" (Aker, 1998, p. 82), they are demonstrating their attention—something about which you can comment at the time or later. Students need to understand your expectations: that is part of creating a genuine learning environment.

Training and practice in questioning

Questioning can be taught as a skill component at any level in the language arts curriculum and as a method of learning in whatever subject areas you are teaching. "Every teacher," Neil Postman reminds us, "regardless of level or subject, must be a language educator" (1979, p. 140).

Training is direct: students learn *about* questioning by practising questioning. James Moffett (1976) writes eloquently about the necessity of teachers understanding that language is only language *when it is being used.* Teachers who instruct students directly as to how and why we question, but do not let them practise are wasting their time and that of their students. Students need to use their knowledge of questioning as they pursue the curriculum.

Here are 12 activities that will allow you and your students to gain direct training in asking questions. The first activity is a means of establishing a partnership between you and your students in designing an environment in which student questioning can flourish.

Building the rules

After a few sessions of talk, students may realize that they need some guidelines. Rules that dictate behavior are more likely to be followed when they have been devised by students themselves. Elementary

Mr. Bugeja urges people to think about why they bought their electronic devices and how they are using them. "If you don't ask and answer those two questions, marketing will. . . . [W]hile the advertising world continues to refine its techniques, we have a moment to think: Where are we going? And when we get there, will we be citizens in the traditional sense of the word at all?"
—Tralee Pearce (2006, p. F8)

classrooms often have these student-generated guidelines on their walls and more rarely, we have seen them in secondary schools.

Here are two we have noticed:

Senior

> Keep the bull for the bull sessions!
> If you haven't got anything to say, don't say it here!
> Don't hog the floor. [illustrated]
> Keep your personal vendettas out of the discussion.
> Don't assume everyone else is a fool but you.
> Keep to the point!
> The opinions expressed here are not food for gossip there.

Elementary

> If everyone speaks at once, no one can hear anything.
> Speak up, listen hard, and take turns.
> THINK before you speak.
> Everybody gets to talk.
> Talk about things that matter.
> WE, in Grade Five, WELCOME YOUR OPINIONS.

Guidelines can be amended as the year goes along.

Discovering what questions do

If you want your students to examine the kinds of thinking that the different forms of questions promote, we suggest that you decide with your students on a specific topic or source.

Once the topic is chosen, have students brainstorm in groups of two or three to make lists of questions on the topic. At the same time, you should build your questions as back-up to cover forms of questions that they may not use, so that all three categories will be put into operation.

Together, analyse the kinds of thinking the questions produce.

EXAMPLE
Topic: Trees
Class: Grade 11 (15/16 years old)

Some examples from the brainstorming:

– What chemical changes in leaves cause them to change color?
– In Pelham [Ontario], they claim to have the largest maple tree in Canada.
– How do they know this?
– I wonder why we so often use trees as metaphors?
– How can I prevent the destruction of the rain forests of the world?

By analysing their own questions, students will see how questions can do more than elicit information. Questions can help them to see a topic or source from different perspectives; help them to explore a variety of attitudes through their responses, and lead them to new questions.

Conducting an inquiry/working scientifically (Brownlie et al., 1988)

First, choose the topic to investigate, and then with the class, make lists (using the chalkboard, overhead projector, or chart paper) under the following headings:

> What do we know about the topic?
> What do we need to know?
> Where can we find the answers?
> Who might help us?

Have students (individuals, pairs, or small groups) conduct research in response to those questions. The following new board headings will emerge:

> What have we learned? (a new version of question 1)
> What new questions do we have? (a new version of question 2)

EXAMPLE
Topic: Honey
Class: Grade 5 (10/11 years old)

What do we know?
– Honey is made by bees.
– There are lots of different kinds of honey.
– It's made from flowers.
– There is a queen bee, little bees and bumble bees.
– It's sweet. It's made in a hive. In a comb.
– It is sometimes runny and sometimes hard.
And so on.

What do we need to know?
– How is honey made?
– Why don't bees get sticky?
– What's the thing about bees and pollen?
– What do they eat when we take the honey?
– Is it better for you than sugar?
– Why is it called a comb?
– Do killer bees make honey?

Where can we find the answers?
– The library—look in the catalogue under bees, insects, honey.
– Books at home
– Honey jar
– Department of Agriculture—Tim's father works for the government.
– Our classroom dictionary
– Television—nature programs

Who might help us?
– Louise's dad. He's a beekeeper.
– Mr. Southern has hives on his property.
– Mr. Prothero (the science teacher)
– Our parents

Upon her deathbed, the great American poet Gertrude Stein is said to have suggested that rather than answers, we should consider, "What is the question?"

The appropriate question, asked at the right moment, can be the key to clarifying communication.

In an examination of the results of lesson study groups, it was noted: "Classroom activities do not challenge students appropriately. In many classes, students are not engaged in learning through the instructional materials . . . that while students were 'compliant, they exhibited little agency.'" And part of the evidence for this was as follows:

- "The level of student interaction in the presence of the text was non-existent."
- "No one was asking the kids to generate the questions."
- "She spent a lot of time on the prompt. She had in her mind what the right answers were—communicated it to the kids. When do you give kids expression of their own voice?"

—Sharon Rallis et al. (2006, p. 544)

After the research was completed, students considered these questions:

What have we learned?
- Killer bees are no different from other bees, just more bad-tempered.
- Ordinary bees don't attack unless disturbed. Killer bees will attack if they feel like it. They are not yet in Canada.
- Louise's dad gave us lots of technical knowledge: how many bees to a hive, how much honey one bee can make, etc.
- My Gran said that honey was better for us than sugar.
- When you take honey out of a hive, you put sugar in for them to eat.
- Now I understand about "busy as a bee."

What new questions do we have?
- Why are some people, like Jeff, so allergic to bee stings?
- Was honey here before sugar?
- What will happen when killer bees come to Canada?
- If honey is more nutritious than sugar, doesn't it harm the bees when we take it away?

And so the process goes on.

This procedure works well using letters, diary or journal entries, photographs, pictures, newspaper clippings, math and science problems and so on, as sources for learning through asking questions.

The ReQuest procedure

This reading strategy was designed by A.V. Manzo (1969) to help students develop an "active inquiring attitude . . . examine alternatives and originate information" (see also Brownlie et al., 1988, pp. 81–86). The teacher asks two or three students to help her ask the class questions about the story they are reading. At the same time as they ask the question, they identify the kind of question as *on the line*, *between the lines*, or *beyond the lines* (which you will remember from Chapter 5).

EXAMPLE
Topic: The story of Little Red Riding Hood
Class: Grade 3 (8/9 years old)

  Q. Mary: Where did Little Red Riding Hood's grandmother live? On the line question
  A. Alice: *That's easy. In a house in the forest. Look at the picture!*
  Q. Jason: What rule did L. R. R. break when the wolf spoke to her? Between the lines
  A. Anne: *She spoke to a stranger.*
  A. Tom: *And she told him where she was going.*
  Q. Teacher: Beyond the line question. I wonder why her mother didn't go with her?

After experiencing this kind of overt training, students should be able to ask these kinds of questions to themselves as they read in the Language Arts program and in all other courses of study.

Study guide questioning

Using questions is an effective way of recalling chalkboard, textbook, or lecture material.

Procedure

The student formulates and writes down the questions for which the material, in his notes or textbook, supplies the answers.

Later, in discussion, reviewing, or preparing for examinations, the student can discover what he knows (or doesn't know) by means of answering his own questions.

EXAMPLE

> When the goal is to "cover" the content, efficiency and accuracy in delivery of information become measures of "effectiveness." If we ask questions we may have to "waste" time correcting inaccuracies in students' responses. If we permit students to ask questions, we may fail to reach our content goals. Yet students' "inaccurate" answers to our questions, and their irrelevant questions to us, reveal the true "effectiveness" of our "delivery system." (Kurfiss, 1989, p. 2)

What is the "content coverage myth" and how does it inhibit learning?

Making up test questions

Another way you can train students to recognize the significance of their learning is to empower them with what is usually viewed as a teacher task: creating test questions. This activity should be seen not as a practice exercise but as a part of the reflection on the unit of study. Sometimes the making of the questions can become the test itself.

The teacher might introduce this activity by saying: "When we are making up tests, we need to ask questions that draw out the information we know, show that we understand the information, and give us opportunities to express our own ideas and opinions about the information."

EXAMPLE
Topic: Political systems
Class: Students in Grade 11 (15/16 years old)

After discussion, these are the questions they agreed upon:

- What are the responsibilities of the upper and lower houses in the democratic system?
- In this country, what conditions might lead to the creation of a totalitarian state?
- Under what political system would you like to hold office?

The students in small groups spent 30 minutes brainstorming the questions. They spent the remaining 30 minutes in discussing, arguing and defending their choices to the rest of the class. This activity revealed to the teacher their knowledge and understanding of this unit of study, served as review, and almost made the test redundant!

We must rediscover how to ask simple questions about ourselves. —John Ralston Saul (1993, p. 36)

Questions breed actions that lead to further questions, and these, in turn, to the boldness of further inquiring acts . . . the living history of man is the story of the questions he has enacted rather than the conclusions he has anchored in science or dogma. —George Kelly (1963, p. 12)

Twenty Questions

This old party game has educative possibilities for questioning training and practice.

Procedure

One or more students choose a specific article (*the sword that Arthur drew from the stone*), person (*Mother Teresa*) or place (*the Parthenon*). The rest of the class are allowed 20 questions, to which the answer must either be "Yes" or "No." They may, at any time, make a direct guess, but if they have not guessed correctly, they have used up one of the 20 questions they are allowed to make. A maximum of three direct guesses is allowed.

The main function of this game is to help students to think carefully in order not to waste questions. For example, in this sequence there is a wasted question:

"Is it male?"
"No."
"Is it female?"

The other function is to help students to narrow the field by asking questions to which a "Yes" or "No" answer provides pertinent information upon which they can build. Compare the alternatives below:

"Is she an athlete?"   "Does she play soccer?"
"Yes."   "No."
"Does she play winter sports?" "Does she play basketball?" . . .
"No."

The first sequence is more effective.

We have found that groups of six, where two students select the topic and four ask questions, offer greater opportunities for students to practise. You can also suggest that your students examine the kinds of questions that are asked on radio and television versions or adaptations of Twenty Questions.

Hot Seating

Twenty Questions is about asking closed questions, something that needs to be balanced by giving students opportunities to make questions that invite the responders to elaborate and originate. In the drama strategy of Hot Seating, the person on the "hot seat" answers questions as a specific person.

Have students form groups of four (A, B, C, D). Member A chooses a person from history, literature, or current events and reveals his choice to the rest of the group. He will be on the "hot seat."

The task of members B, C, and D is to design questions where the focus is on drawing out the respondent's knowledge, experience, imagination, and feelings by requiring him to read between the lines and beyond the lines. Information questions may be asked where appropriate. Students need time to formulate the starter questions. It helps to allow member A to listen in as members B, C, and D formulate their questions so that he can begin to consider his answers.

EXAMPLE

Student A chooses to be Galileo. These are the starter questions formulated by B, C, and D:

> B: In what ways did you change the world?
> C: If you were alive today, where would you like to be and with whom?
> D: What things in your life do you regret?

This exercise is used to help actors develop their stage characters. Fellow actors ask questions that demand that they look more deeply into the meanings behind and beyond the words of the script. If you use Hot Seating simply as questioning practice, Student A would not need to do any preparation other than to sharpen his imagination. Hot Seating used for novel study or in history or science is an excellent way for students to test their understanding of motivation. Here, their answers are built around the material in the text. They are supplemented with appropriate imaginative responses only when no information is available.

Question/Question

This game is played by the protagonists in the opening scene of Tom Stoppard's play *Rosencrantz and Guildenstern Are Dead*. Students gain practice in asking questions by answering each question with a question.

EXAMPLE

> A: Are we going together?
> B: Do you want me to come with you?
> A: Isn't it necessary for both of us to go?
> B: How much do we have to carry?
> A: You don't expect me to help, surely?
> B: Have you forgotten I have a bad back?
> *And so on.*

The rule is that you cannot repeat your partner's question and the guideline is that each question should open up possibilities for your partner (Morgan and Saxton, 1987, p. 104). Paul Bidwell uses this strategy, which he calls "Quescussion," as a way of conducting classroom discussion.

Answer/Question

Bidwell also suggests that an effective means of testing students' knowledge and understanding is to present them with an answer and ask them to provide the questions.

EXAMPLE

> Teacher: The following excerpt is from *A Bird in the House* by Margaret Laurence. For what question or questions might this be the answer?

> I went upstairs to my room. Momentarily, I felt a sense of calm, almost of acceptance. Rest beyond the river. I knew now what that meant. It meant Nothing. It meant only silence forever.

Everything means something. . . .
The question was what.
—Henning Mankell (2004, p. 347)

Then I lay down on my bed and spent the last of my tears, or what seemed then to be the last. Because, despite what I had said to Noreen, it did matter. It mattered, but there was no help for it.
—Margaret Laurence (1978, p. 93)

These questions were among those suggested by members of a senior high school class:

In the story what evidence is there for Vanessa's lack of faith?
What does Vanessa say about death?
What evidence do we have that there has been at least one other event which has caused her to cry?
Is there a part of the story of Vanessa which parallels your own experience?

Role-playing

In any role playing situation, all that is required is that the task and the roles "be done seriously and responsibly as any professional would do it. It is this attention to the task which protects the students from worrying about what they sound or look like."
—Norah Morgan and Juliana Saxton (1987, p. 119)

Role play offers a different way of questioning curriculum content. For example, we can study *Hamlet* by reading the text and answering the teacher's questions or we can build, in role as reporters for *People* magazine, the questions we would need to ask in order to file a "Bio" story. A different aspect of the story would be revealed if Hamlet were questioned by the students in role as psychiatrists. This approach is equally successful with sources from a study novel, textbook, or children's picture book.

Role-playing is not about acting out, acting like, imitating, showing, or even pretending. In role-playing, all that is required of the participant is to see the world through someone else's eyes or, as in Hot Seating, as if he were that person. When in role, the student responds as that person would think and feel, expressing attitudes and points of view in response to situations, relationships, and problems to be solved.

Students have no difficulty in adapting their language to the role because they are used to adapting their language to their changing roles in life. The style, vocabulary, tone, logic, content, and metaphors of language in the home are different from those used with peers. The language of the classroom has its own structure which will change depending upon the content and the teacher, and those students who carry part-time jobs adapt to the particular jargon and style demanded by their employment. Role play in the classroom can offer an infinite number of opportunities to deepen, enrich, and extend language experience by inviting students to explore situations *as if* they were someone else.

There are many games that use question-asking as a means of entertainment. We suggest that you and your students investigate these sources at the public library and game shops to find those which you can adapt for classroom learning.

For example, the way in which senior students interpret a report and question a standing committee on the environment will be quite different if they are in role as environmentalists than if they are in role as industrialists or as the unemployed workers. Junior students, given the opportunity to work in role as parents called in to the school to discuss bullying, will ask different kinds of questions from those they would ask if they were school officials called in to investigate student absenteeism. Kindergarten and primary students are gifted role players, as capable of questioning a king as a bank robber.

Grouping for role-playing: In role play students can work in a variety of ways. For example:

- Put the class into pairs: one student in role as Hamlet is questioned by the other in role as, say, a reporter or psychiatrist.
- The students work in small groups where three reporters or psychiatrists question one person as Hamlet; or one reporter or psychiatrist questions three members of the Danish court about Hamlet.
- The students work as a whole group in which one student in role as Fortinbras questions those in the court as to what has been going on; or, the citizens of Norway can question Fortinbras about the "rotten" state of Denmark.

Similarly, in an elementary social studies class looking at the opening of the American West (O'Neill and Lambert, 1982):

- The whole group as potential emigrants can question the Government Land Agent (the teacher in role).
- A reporter (student) can question the group about why they want to go West and what they hope to find when they get there.
- In pairs, the one who has decided to go can be questioned by one who is still undecided.
- In small groups, a grandchild can question the elders of the family about the journey they took so many years ago.
- A small group of modern-day historians can try to find the true story by questioning some individuals who took that journey.

Notice in this last exercise how the present and the past are brought together. In role play, you can manipulate time which provides another dimension of experience for your students.

Some Roles That Promote Questioning:

The Learner: The questioner wants to know.

The Absentee: The questioner is filling in the gaps.

The Researcher: The questioner wants to find out something specific.

The Interviewer: The questioner is building a picture of the person being interviewed.

The Media Reporter: The questioner is working with the particular bias of his employer which dictates the kinds of questions that are asked.

The Policeman: The questioner is looking for facts; the focus is on what is or was.

The Detective: The questioner is looking for clues; the questions are designed to be indirect and divergent as incongruities are sought out.

The Lawyer: The questioner is building a case; the focus is on winning the case.

The Devil's Advocate: The questioner is challenging the argument, statements, or the story by taking the opposite point of view.

(Morgan and Saxton, 1987, pp. 84–85)

Working in role provides a safety net. It gives students the confidence to express attitudes and points of view that they do not normally hold or may be afraid to express as themselves; it gives them the excitement of challenging their peers and the teacher and, because they are manipulating the material themselves, it provides the added dimension of personal investment in curriculum content. (See Appendix 2: Who Asks Questions?)

Analysing a tape-recording

One of the most effective means of monitoring the development of questioning skills is to use a tape recorder. Students enjoy analysing their questions by this method and so can you. Tell your students that you are using the tape recorder to help you improve your teaching. They, and you, will soon forget about it. Simply turn it on at the beginning of class and off at the end. When you have the time, sit down and listen to it. There are all sorts of things for which you can listen. For example:

- How many questions am I asking?
- Am I using all the categories?
- What variety of questions am I asking?
- Which questions get the students to talk?
- What is the quality of their answers?
- How long is the "thinking time"?
- Are my biases showing?
- Who is doing all the talking?
- How many student questions are there?
- What do I need to work on? Voice? Intonation . . . ?

It takes a little time to get used to listening analytically to yourself—but students don't seem to have the same trouble! If you would prefer, invite a colleague into the classroom. Decide together on a short list of things that he or she will listen for and after the class is over, sit down together and discuss the results. You can do the same for your colleague. We know of a number of teachers who have improved their skills in this way and found it, rather to their surprise, to be an invigorating, as well as useful, experience.

Switching places with your students and working with them as partners to create an active, cooperative learning environment does not mean that you are abrogating your responsibilities as a teacher. Just as the students are taking on different roles so you, too, are adding the roles of facilitator and enabler. Achieving this takes time and practice. You and your students are building a new agenda for teaching and learning. They will come to see you not just as someone who holds answers, but also as someone who, like them, is seeking answers.

Our final chapter is a sample lesson in which the educational focus is to provide opportunities for students to consider the making of questions, to pose those questions, and to face the challenge of having to deal with the answers that their questions engender.

As the quality of the teacher's questions improves, so too does the quality of the students' questions; as the teacher demonstrates that s/he is listening and interested when others are speaking, so do students increase their attentiveness to each other; as teachers accede to, refer to, validates students' ideas—so then does student behaviour begin to change.
—Sondra Napell (In Hawkins, 1976, p. 9)

Once you have learned to ask questions—relevant and appropriate and substantial questions—you have learned how to learn and no one can keep you from learning whatever you need to know.
—Neil Postman and Charles Weingartner (1969, p. 23)

Chapter 12   The Example Lesson: Ann Graham

Jonothan Neelands refers to the source "as a useful case study both of open structure and of the power of student questioning in constructing as narrative." His text, *Structuring Drama Work* (Cambridge University Press, 1990), offers other open structures that invite students into active participation in their learning.

This lesson is modelled on the layout of the story drama structures in *Into the Story: Language in Action through Drama* (Miller and Saxton, 2004). We invite you to teach or adapt this structure to your own and your students' needs.

The format of this lesson, designed by Jonothan Neelands, is an effective means of promoting student questioning skills. You will notice that the strategy—a combination of conducting an inquiry and role playing—enriches the complexity of the task and deepens the intellectual and emotional engagement of the students. The source text has proved to be of great interest to students from junior grades through to post-secondary. Sources appropriate to the interests and experiences of other age groups can function equally well within this format. The lesson as described here was taught over four days in one-hour sessions.

Subject: English.
Class: Grade 11 (15/16 years old)
Type: 30 students—14 boys, 16 girls (mixed ethnic backgrounds)
General Characteristics: The class possesses average ability. Students are eager to work in groups of their own choice. There is a resistance to using language, either orally or in written form. When interested and challenged, students show an ability to think creatively. They have little experience of role playing.
Teacher's Objectives: To provide opportunities for students to ask questions and to listen to questions and answers from their peers; to analyse, classify, and evaluate the effectiveness of those questions; and to write stories based on the information gathered from the questions and answers

> In 1872, the body of Ann Graham was found by the road that runs from Ashtown to Moose Creek, as it passes the farm of Samuel Taylor. Ann, daughter of John, a blacksmith of Ashtown, had left her home some months before. No one spoke of her leaving. No one spoke of her death. No gravestone marks her burial place.

Session 1: Raising questions

1. What can we learn from the source?

Focus: To discover what we know from the source

Grouping: Whole class
Strategy: Deconstructing a source
Administration: Source written out on chart paper
Time: 15 minutes

> Teacher: This morning we are going to explore the ways in which people make stories together—to see what happens when we lay our stories

An alternative source, based on Neelands and designed for elementary students by Norah Morgan, who has used it in more than 20 schools, is as follows:

In the year 2000 Mary Ellery, daughter of William and Elizabeth Ellery, left her home in Mountsville to travel to the planet Osiris. She was a member of the group Venture, led by Dr. James Harvey. Mary never returned. The team does not speak of her. There is no mention of her in the records and her name does not appear in the medal citation which honors the work of Dr. Harvey and his group.

Grouping: Groups of 5
Strategy: Finding questions and assumptions
Administration: 6 sheets of chart paper; 6 felt pens
Time: 20 minutes

alongside other people's. This means that we are all going to listen very carefully so that no one imposes a story on the story we are *all* making. Let me be very clear about one thing, the story we make *is* the story. Don't come up to me at the end and say, "Yes, but now tell us the *real* story" because the real story is the one we will make. All we have to build our story from is this fragment.

The teacher puts up the text on the board.

Teacher: Just read this fragment quietly to yourselves. (*The students do so.*) What do we know from reading this fragment?

Some examples of answers:

Student A: Ann Graham died on the road to Ashtown.
Student B: We don't know she died there. Her body was found there.
Student A: You're right!
Student C: Her father was a blacksmith.
Student D: She must have died under strange circumstances because no one spoke of her death.
Student E: We don't know that; people may not have spoken about it because they lived in a community of deaf and dumb people!
Student B: It doesn't read like that. If it were normal, no one would have written it like that.
And so on.

2. What questions do we have here?

Focus: To sort out assumptions from facts; to work collectively; to build a list of questions that are useful, well phrased, designed to elicit information, and congruent with the period of the source

Teacher: We really don't know very much, do we? What questions are beginning to form in your mind? Groups of five, please. Take a sheet of chart paper and one felt pen per group. Appoint a secretary to record your questions. (*They do so.*)
Beware of swamping other people's ideas with your own. We are working out of the facts we have and any logical assumptions that arise from those facts. You have about five minutes, so get moving!

Students work well discussing, arguing about the relevance, the wording and the importance of the questions. The teacher stands aside and reminds them of time passing (which turns out to be closer to 10 minutes than 5).

Teacher: Right everyone. Stop there. Let's hear what we've got from each group in turn. Who's ready to begin? (*Group A so indicates.*)

Questions are shared. The teacher records those questions that the class agrees upon on the board, next to the source. Some examples:

Group A: How many months was Ann pregnant?
(This question is almost always first to be asked.)
Teacher: Be careful! You are imposing your own story. We don't know enough yet to make an assumption like that. Can you word the question another way so that that information could be revealed?
Group A: Was Ann pregnant?

Group C: No, that's still not right. We've got a better one! What was the condition of Ann's health?

Group D: We don't know how old she was. We have, "How old was Ann at the time of her death?"

Teacher: What do you want me to write down?

Group B: Put down the one about her age first and then the one about her health.

Teacher: Are we agreed that both will be useful questions? (*They agree.*)

This sharing continues until 15 questions that the whole class agrees are useful are on the board. Throughout, the teacher gives careful consideration to how the questions are phrased. Some examples:

- Is there another way of putting that so that it will open up the inquiry rather than close it down?
- Can we write that another way so that it gets at what we want to know more directly? Remember we want to keep the story very open at this point.
- Try not to follow one story line but rather, make these questions so that they cover a breadth of "territory."

3. Who holds the answers to these questions?

Focus: To build a collective list of the people who might help us to learn more about the story

Grouping: Whole class
Strategy: Discussion
Administration: Groups' questions, felt pen
Time: 20 minutes

Teacher: Read the questions carefully. Who might be able to answer them?

The class offers suggestions:
- Ann's father
- Samuel Taylor
- The religious adviser (*Students are concerned that a religion not be specified yet.*)
- A hairdresser

A student objects, "No! That isn't right with the period."

An argument ensues.

Teacher: What I'm hearing is that you want to speak to someone who's in a position to know what's going on in the community.

The students first decide on a barber.
- The barber
- The doctor
- Ann's best friend

The teacher rejects a suggestion of Ann's lover as being "I" writing rather than "we" writing—"Remember we are building a *collective* story."
- The person who found the body
- The person who buried her

As the roles are approved, they are listed on the board beside the 15 questions.

Teacher: Now we have eight people who might be able to give us some answers that would help us to build our story. As you think about what has happened today, be careful not to build a story of your own. Remember, the story we are building is one that must belong to all of us. Thank you for your hard work.

Session 2: Building a story through questioning

4. Reconnecting with the source

Focus: To review previous day's information and set the tone for serious work

Grouping: Whole class
Strategy: Silent reading
Administration: The board questions and roles list are transcribed onto chart paper and pinned up beside the source text.
Time: 5 minutes

Depending upon the students' interest, this part of the lesson may take two classes.

> Teacher: Please reread the source that we have been investigating and examine the questions we developed and the people we decided might be able to provide answers. We need to have this information at our fingertips as this is going to be a very demanding lesson. (*Students do as directed. There is some quiet conversation while they are reading.*)

5. Who will we talk to now and how are we going to do it?

Focus: To be sure that each student knows "what's up"

Grouping: Whole class—divided
Strategy: Organizing or "setting the stage"; pencils and paper for the scribes; enough chairs for each student
Administration: 25 chairs set in a circle
Time: 5 minutes

> Teacher: We need to deepen our understanding of the events surrounding the death of Ann Graham and for that I am going to invite five volunteers. Each volunteer will take on the responsibility of representing one of the roles we have listed on the board. (*Five students offer.*)
>
> Thank you. I am going to ask you to stand apart from us and not to talk to each other. And, while I know that you are prepared to undertake one of the roles listed, please do not make that choice now. I will tell you what we are going to do in a moment.

The teacher turns to class.

> Teacher: Now, we need to record the questions that we ask of those who are representing the roles on our board list. Do I have five volunteers to be scribes? (*Five students volunteer.*) Great!
>
> The rest of you, please arrange your chairs in a circle. Scribes, please get paper and a pencil from my desk and then, take your chairs and set them just outside the circle. (*They do.*)
>
> Let me just talk to the scribes for a moment. Mary, you record the questions addressed to George; Allan, you write the questions we ask Jane. (*And so on until each scribe is assigned one of the role players.*)

The teacher then places five chairs randomly within the circle, facing in different directions.

> Teacher (to the role players): You will come in when you are called and sit on any chair you choose. Once you sit, you are in role. Do not decide which role you will take now but, rather, make up your mind as you are coming in to sit down among us. You will need to listen very carefully to each interview and decide what you will agree with as a fact and when you can offer another point of view. For example, if Ann's father were to be interviewed and tells us that Ann's mother died in childbirth, that would be a fact that would become a part of the story. However, if the barber says that Ann's father is a "skinflint" that is something that someone else might dispute.
>
> The reason why I ask you not to decide on your role beforehand is because as the interviews proceed, you may see that one role from our list of roles, rather than another, would be more helpful to building the story.

Teacher (to everyone): We are ready now to question. We will all have to listen carefully to the answers we are given because it is upon those answers that we build our story. Remember that these people have *agreed* to speak to us. I know you will treat them with respect.

6. Who will we meet and what will they tell us?

Focus: To develop questioning skills; to fold new information into old; to encourage focused listening; to work in role

Teacher (to the students sitting in the circle): Thank you for coming today to try and solve the mystery of Ann Graham's death. We are here to find the truth and we have all signed the form not to publish our findings without permission.

This speech suggests a general role to the students which sets a loose context for asking the questions.

Teacher: It is important to remember that the event we are investigating happened 10 years ago. There will be details that our guests will be unable to remember, things that they simply do not wish to talk about, and things which they cannot talk about.

Using a gesture only, the teacher invites someone in the "role" group to come forward into the circle and sit down in one of the chairs set out previously.

Teacher: Thank you for coming. May I ask your name and your relationship to or connection with Ann Graham?

An example of the procedure:

Student (in role): My name is John Graham. I am Ann's father.
Teacher: We know you might find some of our questions distressing and that you may have forgotten some of the details of that time 10 years ago. We will understand if you do not wish to answer all the questions. This is not an inquisition. Who has the first question for Mr. Graham?

The teacher follows a similar format with the other four students who choose to take on the roles of Samuel Taylor, the barber, a nun at the convent where Ann attended school, and the person who buried her. While they are being questioned, the students in role are not to interact with one another. When Samuel Taylor makes a derogatory comment about John Graham and John Graham turns to say something, the teacher intervenes immediately, saying, "We are speaking to Mr. Taylor."

There are about ten questions asked of each role player although the barber has fewer questions because he tends to gossip more and the nun has more questions because she answers only what is asked of her. Of the 61 questions asked, the teacher makes six question interventions: two questions for clarification, one question because she is intrigued and needs to know for herself, and three questions in order to open up the questioning or change the pattern of the asking.

Some examples of student questions and comments on them:

To Mr. Graham: What was your relationship with Samuel Taylor?
Comment: A good open question providing a number of pieces of information upon which others build their questions

---

Grouping: 5 class members, 5 scribes, 20 class members
Strategy: Questioning in role
Administration: As set out above
Time: 20 minutes

Is the point of curriculum the mastery of information that may become quickly outdated, or is curriculum content the vehicle to teach students to understand, value, reflect, and create? Is curriculum about providing marketable skills—assuming such a market exists—or opening minds? Should the individual's potential or the progress of the group receive priority?
—Heather Jane Robertson (1998, p. 5)

To the nun: And what was Ann's home life like?
Comment: This question invites the nun to support or oppose what a previous speaker has implied. The nun responds, "I am not in a position to speak of those things," which is a more powerful answer than had she answered the question directly.

To the barber: What do you think of Samuel Taylor?
Comment: The student who asks this question wants information, but the way the question is worded gives the barber licence to be creative with his answer which tells us a great deal about the barber, a little about Taylor and nothing at all about Ann's death. When the students later analyse the questions, the teacher uses this question to demonstrate the importance of phrasing.

To Samuel Taylor: We understand from Mr. Jackson, the barber, that you have a son?
Student in role: Yes.
Student questioner: What are your ambitions for him?
Comment: This exchange comes late in the interview with Mr. Taylor. The first question is asked to check that the information previously given is correct; the second question is the key question which begins to unravel the mystery.

The last student to be questioned by the large circle is a girl.

Teacher: I know we've kept you waiting a long time. Thank you for your patience. What is your name?
Student in role: Mrs Jenkins.
Teacher: Mrs Jenkins, might I ask your connection with Ann?
Student in role: I buried her.
A student (*quickly*): How come a woman is burying the dead?
(That question drew the story off into an interesting direction.)

At the end of the questioning:

Teacher (to the circle of questioners): I expect that now there are other questions in your mind which you would like to ask.

7. Checking out the story

Focus: To ask the questions not yet asked; to check out the facts that do not seem to be consistent; to weave the story more tightly

Teacher: These people (*indicating the five students on chairs in the centre of the circle*) will remain in role. You (*to other students*) may go around and ask them any other questions that you may have.
Scribes, this is now your chance to ask questions.

The group breaks up, moving around among the chairs in the centre of the circle, asking questions or just listening to others asking questions. About 10 minutes pass.

Teacher: Thank you. We have no wish to tire these people out. They have been so kind and patient putting up with our questions. You have given us a lot to think about.

Grouping: 5 students in role; the rest of the class
Strategy: Questioning
Administration: As above
Time: 10 minutes

8. What did we hear?

Grouping: Whole class
Strategy: Sharing
Administration: Large circle of chairs
Time: 5 minutes

Focus: To share what has been learned; to evaluate its importance; to try and fit it into the story that is developing

> Teacher (to the role players): Please, come out of role now and may I ask you to bring your chairs back into the large circle. (*They do.*)
>
> Scribes, hang on to your questions for the moment, we may need them as reference. Please, open the circle to let the scribes join us. (*They do.*)
>
> Has anyone picked up any new information which you feel you should share with us?

Many interesting things are mentioned, phrased in ways such as these:

- I learned that . . .
- I don't understand why her . . .
- Mr. Taylor seemed uncomfortable about . . .
- I think we should all know that . . .

9. Laying Ann to rest

Grouping: Whole class
Strategy: Setting a scene; tapping in
Administration: As described below
Time: 10 minutes

Focus: To place students in the middle of the story; to demonstrate multiple perspectives of an event

> Teacher: Scribes, please put your recorded questions on my desk. Thank you. Everyone, please place all the chairs *but one* against the walls and stand by them.

The teacher takes the remaining chair, turns it over and places it on the floor in the middle of the room.

> Teacher: This chair marks the spot where Ann Graham's body is to be buried. Will those of you who took on roles, please place yourselves *where* you would be and *how* you would be at the time of Ann's burial. (*They do so.*)

The rest of the class watches as the picture takes shape.

> Teacher: Look at this picture. If there is anything you don't understand about the arrangement, ask a question.

Some examples:

> Student: Bill, why are you standing on that chair?
> Bill: I don't think Taylor would be at the burial, but I am standing on my hill, watching.

Students question until everyone is satisfied with the picture.

> Teacher (to the rest of the class): Now it is your turn. As members of Ann's village, take a moment to think where you might be and what you might be doing at the moment of Ann's burial. (*She waits.*)
>
> Now, you will take your place in the picture one at a time. (*They do, in silence.*)
>
> Just hold that picture for a moment. Close your eyes.
>
> The body is now being lowered into the ground. What question is in your mind? I shall come around and place my hand on your shoulder. When you feel my hand, say your question aloud.

Tapping In

Teacher moves through the group, placing a hand on each participant's shoulder and asking a question such as, "Tell me what you are thinking?" "What are your concerns?" Keep your hand, gently but firmly, on the participant's shoulder until you are sure the statement has been completed.
—Carole Miller and Juliana Saxton (2004b, p. 160)

Some examples (6 of 26; 4 students passed):

- What was in Ann's mind the moment she faced death?
- Why am I not allowed to toll the bell?
- Why didn't I do what I knew I should have done?
- She asked for it. What's all the fuss about?
- I wonder what the person who killed her is thinking now?
- *The final question was a single word—Why?*

Teacher leaves a silence.

10. What now?

Focus: To consider the story they have made together; to think about how they made the story and what helped it to grow

Grouping: Pairs or threes
Strategy: Reflection
Administration: None
Time: As long as needed

Teacher: Just find someone near to you, sit down together and when you are ready, begin talking about the experience. (*They do.*)

After students have reflected together and shared their thinking,

Teacher: We have been building a collective story, but there are still many questions to be answered. Now it is time for you to write about the story as *you* see it. Hold to the facts that have been established but you are free to tell the story in your own way. You may write it as a diary entry, a letter, a short story, a newspaper article, as the summary of a trial—in any way that you feel is right for what you want to say and how you want to say it. I expect you to have your first draft ready for next class.

Session 3: Writing based on information gathered

11. What really happened?

Focus: To work collaboratively, to read their own words or those of another aloud or silently, to assess, to edit, to rewrite

Grouping: Pairs or small groups
Strategy: Composing; editing; discussion
Administration: First drafts; a place to work by themselves for those who "forget"
Time: 60 minutes and time outside of class

This composition lesson fulfills the third teaching expectation: to provide opportunities for students to write stories based on the information gathered from the questions and answers.

Students write in pairs or small groups, sharing their first drafts and working as editors with their partners. None of the students completes the assignment in class time. Their completed writings are handed in later, indicating their commitment to the task and to the work of the previous lessons.

The writings took many forms: some assignments were on paper made to look old, some were letters (one or two sealed with wax), one was in the form of Samuel Taylor's will, a number were written as diary entries, and some were short stories.

Session 4: Examining how questions helped build the story

12. Analysing our questions

Grouping: Groups of four (two absentees)
Strategy: Analysis
Administration: A selection of 8 to 10 transcribed questions that demonstrate the categories; question categories on board with identifying letter, pencils; response sheets for each group (see Appendix 5)
Time: 15 minutes

Focus: To provide opportunities for students to analyse, classify, and evaluate the effectiveness of the questions (second teaching expectation)

> Teacher: I have here the scribes' transcriptions of the questions that you asked or were asked during the in-role interviews. Each group will have the list of questions that were asked and a response sheet. Your first task is look at the questions and decide which questions fit under the headings that are on the board. Record your decision on the response sheet. You'll note that I have given each type of question a letter for easy identification. Questions that give us information are type A. Questions that draw answers to fill in the gaps between the facts and help us make connections are type B. Questions that invite answers that deepen the story are type C.

> *Students work with the questions.*

13. Valuing and rephrasing questions

Grouping: Groups of four
Strategy: Evaluation; editing; rewriting
Administration: As above
Time: 10 minutes

Focus: To consider how a question works and how a question might be more effectively phrased

> Teacher: Now, thinking as writers, talk together about how each question helped us to build our story. Write your decision on the response paper. Finally, if you feel that the question would work better if it were rephrased, use the space for rephrasing or to comment on why the question did not need rephrasing.

> *The teacher circulates while students work.*

> Teacher: You have some good ideas. Let's share some of our work. In your group, choose an example that you would like to share with us. Tell us the question, what kind of question you decided it was, how it helped the story and, if you thought of a better way to put the question. (*They make their choices.*)
>
> As we listen to these questions, think about the quality of the question, how the words are put together to invite an answer and which ones invite you to answer.

> *A number of questions are shared and discussed. There is a lively discussion about whether the questions made connections or deepened the story. Students conclude that, as writers, they see the value of the question lies in the connections it makes but, as readers, they feel the answer works to deepen the story. The teacher asks for the revised question sheets to be put on her desk. She later reviewed these sheets to identify if any re-teaching needed to be done.*

14. The big questions that remain to be asked

Grouping: Pairs
Strategy: Composing
Administration: Enough paper for students; pencils or pens
Time: 10 minutes

Focus: To encourage students to think beyond the story in new ways

> Teacher: Find a partner. (*They do.*) Take a moment to sit quietly and think. Stories, if they are to reach a wide audience, have something in them that is universal. If you had the opportunity to ask not more than three "big"

questions that would help us to see this story as more than just Ann Graham's story, what might those questions be? Who might be able to answer them?

Work together and share your ideas. (*They do.*)

As students work, the teacher circulates. After a time warning, she asks students to find another pair and share their work. They do. A few minutes pass.

Teacher: There are some wonderful questions here that really open up the story in quite unexpected ways. Let's hear some of them.

Some examples:

- Some say it would have been better if she had never been born. How do you see her life and death?
- If no one ever really loved Ann, what kind of mother could she have been if her baby had lived?
- Is something less wrong simply because it happened in the past?

The whole class then moved into a discussion prompted by the question "Why are some questions difficult to answer?"

Raising difficult questions

The questions that the students raised are indeed difficult to answer. As with most questions of this nature, no answers were forthcoming, but reflecting on them created a discourse that was thoughtful, attentive, aware, and rich in perspectives. In an increasingly complex world where meanings hold more and more ambiguities, not finding answers is as important as finding the questions. Once found, we need to know how to think and talk about them together. Only then can we begin to see the breadth of possibilities and implications as we hear and take into consideration others' expressions and points of view. These ways of thinking, listening, and exchanging ideas are central to an effective democratic process.

All people in a democracy are entitled to exercise their rights as citizens. If we do not give our students the tools and the confidence to do so, we are failing to keep the practices of democracy connected to education—something about which many thoughtful people are becoming concerned (Kahne and Westheimer, 2006). Hard questions, effective questioning skills, and many opportunities in the classroom to exercise curiosity are powerful ways to renew our commitment to democracy.

He that questioneth much shall learn much, and content much; but especially if he apply his questions to the skill of the person whom he asketh; for he shall give them occasion to please themselves in speaking and himself shall continually gather knowledge . . .
—Sir Francis Bacon (1561–1626)

Ken Buford, author and cook, talks in *Heat* about how, over time, he began to know when food was cooked, not because the clock said so, but because his nose told him. Later, he writes, he wasn't conscious of the smell, but just knew intuitively that something was ready. The ability to know what and how to ask your questions will, we assure you, develop over time as you discover the power of your questions to make a lesson cook in ways that make teaching and learning more engaging and exciting for you and your students. Then you will know that, as Frances Mayes (1996, p. 124) puts it, "there is only the way to do it. Now, are we going to measure or are we going to cook?" *Bon appétit!*

Appendixes

1: Differences between social talk, classroom discourse and discussion

2: Who asks questions?

3: Building questions upon questions

4: Thinking as someone else

5: Evaluating questions on Ann Graham

6: Questioning behaviors

7: Changing perspectives in the classroom

8: Getting started: A thinking process for teachers

Differences between Social Talk, Classroom Discourse and Discussion

Social Talk	Discourse	Discussion
Definition: Unstructured, informal talk	Informal, but with a flexible structure and generally centred around a topic theme. Inconclusive, though points for further investigation are identified	Formally structured exchange of ideas, dependent upon analysis, synthesis and valuing, moving towards a conclusion to provide a platform for further identified investigations.
Time Frame: None	Dictated by timetable and class time	Generally defined as part of lesson plan
Leader: No leader	Teacher as arbitrator, reference point and administrator	Teacher, unless a student is specified
Grouping: Flexible as people come and go, depending upon their interest	No one can leave and no one joins in unless invited. Participants opt in or out, intellectually and emotionally. Large group can subdivide. Teacher moves about.	Formal large group or assigned smaller groups. Teacher generally central to the discussion (physically)
Point completion: Rarely completed verbal points; many interruptions	More attention given to completing points, fewer interruptions, though they are acceptable	Each contributor completes his thoughts unless he is rambling at which point leader can intervene.
Agenda: No agenda is planned and anyone can introduce a topic which lives or dies according to the interest of the participants.	Topic can be student- or teacher-initiated and students share major responsibility in organization and control of the interaction. Generally, discourse takes the form of generating a context for subject material or reflecting on the work.	Topic and procedure set by the teacher at initiation of the discussion. Procedure is controlled by the leader. The discussion is based on a previous subject experience or external stimulus (play, novel, experiment, etc.).

Note: Social talk can move into discussion when someone has specific knowledge in which others are interested. Discourse, too, can move into discussion if the teacher senses an interest and feels the contributions need to be organized in a more formal manner.

On Conducting Discussion

It may sound trite to say so, but for our democracy to be revitalized, frank and open discussion must be made the order of the day.
—Roy Romanow (2006, p. 52)

Ferrara (1981, p. 71) says that "discussion . . . is a most difficult and demanding process. It involves people as well as ideas; it is social as well as intellectual and a balance must be maintained between the two. The discussion leader must learn to listen, to question and to enjoy the process itself." Teachers often see their place in a discussion as the asker of questions, but discussion demands an exchange of ideas and so students, too, have a right to express their ideas in the form of questions. The questions that they ask will help the teacher to know what they need to learn. The teacher's role in a discussion is that of an "impartial provocateur who assists the group to engage in the subject as comprehensively as possible" (Ambrosino, n.d., p. 18): to put the class at ease, to encourage the talk, to maintain respect for the process, to conclude gracefully and to review immediately. In reviewing, the teacher should note who spoke and what they spoke about.

A Model for Discussion

The private motivation of joining in a discussion is a conscious attempt to sort out with other people matters we recognize as too difficult and complex for anyone to sort out alone.
—Aidan Chambers, (1996, p. 17)

1 Have your question(s) ready. One good question should be enough to generate discussion.
2 Be clear about your expectations and share them with the class.
3 Introduce the topic, develop an outline and try to stick to it. Consider using the chalkboard or chart paper.
4 Ask the class for their reactions to the source material in order to generate some common ground and identify individual concerns, relate these to the topic and the outline and, with the agreement of the students, establish the focus.
5 Explore the topic: this step can appear untidy as things are being sorted out. There are some specific jobs that the teacher can undertake:
   – Watch for personal storying or irrelevancies and intervene to refocus.
   – Keep an eye on the relationship of the variety of ideas to the focus and the outline.
   – Keep an eye on the passage of time.
   – Watch for time-consuming and fruitless arguments.
   – Encourage everyone to participate and to share ideas and experiences; deflect those who start to dominate the discussion.
   – Help students understand by moving their frames of reference from self to seeing from other perspectives.
   – Close off something when it has been sufficiently discussed.
6 Conclude by summing up the flow of the discussion.
7 Invite suggestions for further action and volunteers for further responsibilities.

The notes above are based on research by Charles Ferrara (1981); R. E. Lefton, K. R. Buzzotta, M. Shenburg (1980); S. Ambrosino (n.d.); W. J. McKeachie (1978); and John Norman (1987).

Whether a discussion is teacher or student led, the teacher is responsible for the outcomes. Remember that feelings expressed in discussion are neither right nor wrong; they just are. Mutual acceptance of feelings paves the way for accommodation to others' attitudes and points of view.

Who Asks Questions? Teacher's Notes

Jack and Jill went up the hill
to fetch a pail of water.
Jack fell down and broke his crown
and Jill came tumbling after.

Grouping: Whole class
Strategy: Discussion
Administration: Nursery rhyme on board or chart paper; pencils and response sheets
Focus: Looking for questions that generate rich answers

If some students are unfamiliar with this rhyme, you may need to do some preparatory work. It is always interesting to consider the word "crown," which has different meanings. The royal one is the more interesting for younger children. It is a good idea to decide together which meaning would be the most interesting to follow.

Teacher: Here is the situation: the children are in hospital; they are in satisfactory condition, but they are not allowed to have any visitors yet.
To whom could we speak in order to find out what happened?
Students and teacher make a list.
Now that we have our list, what sorts of questions would we have for each of these people?
Students talk about how those questions would change, depending upon who was asking them and to whom they were talking.
In groups of three, set your chairs in a circle. (*They do.*)
Decide on the person you want to interview. (*They do.*)
Choose someone in your group to respond in that role. (*They do.*)
Decide together who would be asking the questions. (*They do.*)
Think for a moment about the attitudes and points of view of the roles you all have decided upon. Those attitudes and points of view help you form your questions and shape your replies. For example, if we were a group of social workers who think that the rhyme tells a story of unsupervised children, how would that change or color the questions we ask and how we ask them?
When you are ready, you may begin.
The teacher circulates, listening for questions that generate rich responses.
Stop now. Just think quietly about what you have heard. (*They do.*)

Reflection prompts: What sorts of questions did you find to be the most useful?
Who heard something that they hadn't thought of?
Who found themselves surprised by what they were saying?

Extension: You might take the story of Hansel and Gretel. Share it so that everyone agrees on the story's main events. Use the same framework as above, or have the class in role as the People for Better Parents group whose members speak to one or both of the children about best practices in parenting.

Who Asks Questions? Response Form

Here is a list of people whose business it is to ask questions. You may add to this list if you find others.

interviewer	inquisitor
journalist	devil's advocate
doctor	teacher
lawyer	shopkeeper
police officer	psychiatrist/psychologist
detective	children
researcher	politicians (depending on which side of the House they sit)
someone who has been away	social worker
interrogator	conscience
alien	others? _____

1. In this list of roles, who asks questions to which they already know the answer?

_____

_____

2. What might be some reasons that cause people to ask questions to which they already know the answer?

_____

_____

3. Here is a question that we ask every day: "So, what have you been up to?" Choose three people from the list above and decide how each would phrase that everyday question to discover what they need to know.

Example: Shopkeeper: Hello, Mrs. Jones. I haven't seen you for some time. Been away?

Role: _____ Question: _____

_____

Role: _____ Question: _____

_____

Role: _____ Question: _____

_____

4. Remember the story of Cinderella? If you had only three questions you could ask, what would they be and of whom would you ask them?

Question: _____

_____ Name: _____

Question: _____

_____ Name: _____

Question: _____

_____ Name: _____

Building Questions upon Questions: Teacher's Notes

Here, students are both question askers and question responders. Their engagement and their learning will be deepened because they are driving the explorations for themselves. The activities are introduced from the teacher's viewpoint.

Preparation:

The class reads a novel, poem, play, or short story, or views a film, documentary, or a piece of art.

Activity 1 Using your response sheet, write down three questions that you would like answered about this material. (**Task 1**)

Activity 2 With a partner, try to answer each other's questions.

Activity 3 With your partner, decide on three questions for which you would both like to find the answers. You may use questions you already have, or perhaps there are new questions that you have because of your conversation. (**Task 2**)

Activity 4 Each pair joins with another pair. Exchange questions and give your answers.

Activity 5 In your group of four, settle on one question that you all feel is powerful enough to engage the whole class in discussion. When you have decided, choose someone to come up and write it on the board. (**Task 3**)

Activity 6 Now, we have a great list of questions. Where shall we begin our discussion?

The questions generate a reflective discussion that serves both to deepen understanding of the material and offer opportunities for re-teaching, if needed. Although what the questions open up for discussion is more important (Activity 7), you might also explore with the students the criteria on which they based their choices of powerful questions (Activity 8).

Activity 7 Using your response sheet, take a moment to reflect on any changes in your thinking about the material (*reflecting on meaning*).

Activity 8 Write about what you think makes a powerful question (*reflecting on process*).

Adapted from R. McTeague, *Shared Reading in the Middle and High School Years* (Portsmouth, NH: Heinemann, 1992), p. 52.

Building Questions upon Questions: Response Form

Task 1: List your three questions below.

Question 1:

_____

_____

Question 2:

_____

_____

Question 3:

_____

_____

Task 2: List the three questions that you and your partner have decided upon.

Question 1:

_____

_____

Question 2:

_____

_____

Question 3:

_____

_____

Task 3: Write the powerful question that your group has decided upon.

_____

_____

Reflection: How has your thinking changed?

_____

_____

_____

What makes a question powerful?

_____

Thinking as Someone Else: Teacher's Notes

"Thinking as Someone Else" uses some of the questions that actors ask themselves when they are beginning to work on a play. The questions help create the background and context and generate thinking more deeply about how and why things have happened, are happening, or could happen. This exercise uses all the categories of questioning to enable actors to think about their roles, to fill in the gaps, and to see what choices they can try out in order to deepen their roles.

"Thinking as Someone Else" can be used in a variety of subject areas to help students think about the attitudes and points of view that the people involved might hold, for example, thinking as Mme. Curie about the personal costs of scientific discovery. Thinking not just about a subject, but as someone who undertakes that profession or took part in those events is one way that students can master a subject.

How to use the response sheet:

- Students choose their roles. More than one student may take on the same role.
- Begin by answering only a few questions. You and your students can decide on the ones that they can or want to answer.
- When the work is in progress, students will know more and so will be able to answer more questions.
- When the work is completed, it is useful to have students reread what they have written and make any changes that they have in light of their experiences.
- Writing in role (18) is a means of reflecting inside the work and can be done at any time during the work, at the end of the process, or at both times. It may be done in many ways: personal thoughts in a diary; letter to an authority or a friend; letter to the newspaper; stream of consciousness, and so on. How it is done can depend on the situation that promotes it. For example, in role as villagers, student could write a poem mourning the loss of their dear friend, Snow White. (See Chapter 4.) Depending on their skills or the focus, students could write as individuals or as a class.

Thinking as Someone Else: Response Form

Writing in role

1. My name is _____

2. Where do I live? _____

3. What period of time am I living in? _____

4. How old am I in years? in experience? _____
   _____

5. What do I do in my life? _____
   _____

6. What is the central problem for me? _____
   _____

7. What is the central problem for others? _____
   _____

8. Besides my own, whose story is this? _____
   _____

9. What do I want now? in the future? _____
   _____

10. What are my reasons for wanting these things? _____
    _____

11. How shall I get what I want? _____
    _____

12. What can I do to make this happen? _____
    _____

13. Who can help me? _____
    _____

14. How may other people see me? _____
    _____

15. How do I view the world and my place in it? _____
    _____

Thinking as Someone Else: Response Form (continued)

16. What question still needs to be asked about me? _____

_____

17. My answer: _____

_____

18. Writing in role: _____

_____

_____

_____

_____

_____

_____

_____

_____

_____

_____

_____

_____

_____

_____

_____

Writing out of role

19. In what ways is the role like me? _____

_____

20. In what ways is the role different from me? _____

_____

Evaluating Questions on Ann Graham: Teacher's Notes

In Session 4 of the Ann Graham lesson unit (see Chapter 12), the teacher asks students to evaluate on the response sheets the questions that were scribed during the in-role interviews. Students were given five tasks:

1. To look at the questions transcribed and decide what kinds of questions they are:
   - questions that elicit information—A
   - questions that draw out answers that fill in the gaps between the facts and help them make connections—B
   - questions that invite answers that deepen the story—C
2. To select three (or more) questions to examine more closely
3. To decide the category for each question
4. To decide how each question chosen helps build the story
5. To consider if the question could be rephrased in order to elicit a richer response and, if so, to rephrase it

> **Example:** *Mr. Taylor, what was your relationship with Ann's father?*
> **Question Category:** B
> **How did the question help us?** The fact that Mr. Taylor and Mr. Graham didn't get along made Ann's death near his farm more significant.
> **Rephrase?** Good question. Helped us find the plot line. No rephrase needed.

> **Example** (to the barber): *You know a lot about what goes on in this village. Was Ann's mother a witch?*
> **Question Category:** A
> **How did the question help us?** It didn't. The barber only got upset that he was being called a gossip and refused to answer.
> **Rephrase?** Yes, option provided: There was a lot of talk about Ann's mother and her religious practices. I wonder if you heard anything that might help us understand what happened?

Note: The response sheet has room for three questions only. If students are to analyse more, each group will need multiple response pages.

Evaluating Questions on Ann Graham: Response Form

Members of Group: _____

_____

_____

Question: _____

_____

Category _____

How did the question help us? _____

_____

Rephrase?   Yes _____   No _____

Rephrase _____

_____

_____

Question: _____

_____

Category _____

How did the question help us? _____

_____

Rephrase?   Yes _____   No _____

Rephrase _____

_____

_____

Question: _____

_____

Category _____

How did the question help us? _____

_____

Rephrase?   Yes _____   No _____

Rephrase _____

_____

_____

Questioning Behaviors

Below is an example of teacher questioning that comes from *The Self-Directed Theatre: Managing the Learning Process* (Nunan and Lamb, 1996, pp. 80, 81). After you have read it, take a moment to jot down your thoughts in the spaces provided.

> T: Remember. What was happening last week? What just started last week in the video? There was a race, right?
>
> S: Yes.
>
> T: And where was the race?
>
> S: Qu . . . quarry.
>
> T: In the quarry, that's right. There was a race in the quarry. Between two people. A race between . . . which two people?
>
> S: Between Mike.
>
> T: Between Mike and . . . remember?
>
> S: And the college student.
>
> T: And the college student. Remember?
>
> S: Rod.
>
> T: Rod. Remember. Catherine's old boyfriend. So Mike and Rod have started a race. You make a prediction. Who did you think would win the race?
>
> S: [Inaudible]
>
> T: You thought Mike. Who did you think?

Reflections:

What kind of questioning is going on? _____

_____

What sorts of questions are being used? _____

_____

What prompts do you see? _____

_____

What do you think might be going on in the mind of the teacher?

_____

_____

What do you think might be going on in the mind of the student?

_____

_____

What does this example help you to understand about your own questions and questioning?

_____

_____

_____

Changing Perspectives in the Classroom

Sometimes, it is useful to think about what is happening in our classrooms from a different set of perspectives. Here are some questions and question statements that may help you think about your own classroom from "both sides of the desk." It is helpful for later reflection, to identify the time of year; often the same activity will offer different responses depending upon the time of the day that is reflected upon.

Time frame for the reflection: _____

Optional:
Class: _____

Teaching focus: _____

A. Look at your teaching from the students' point of view.
The experience

- ❏ was so good that I want to bring my friends
- ❏ was okay, certainly better than a lecture
- ❏ was boring but necessary
- ❏ had nothing to do with me
- ❏ none of the above, but . . .

When I look at my teacher, I see someone who

- ❏ is really interested in the material and in helping me to understand
- ❏ is scared of us
- ❏ is bored by us
- ❏ has lots of energy
- ❏ really sees me
- ❏ is interesting to look at

When I listen to my teacher, I

- ❏ am entertained but nothing stays with me
- ❏ hear stories that help me to relate to the material
- ❏ hear stories that help me to understand the material
- ❏ hear stories that have nothing to do with anything that I can see
- ❏ hear background noise

When my teacher walks into the room, I feel

- ❏ a sense of anticipation
- ❏ confident that I can deal with whatever comes up
- ❏ that whatever happens will be important to me
- ❏ I will probably be wasting my time, but what can I do about it?
- ❏ a sense of impending doom!

When my teacher asks questions, I feel

- ❏ she already knows the answer
- ❏ there is only one right answer
- ❏ she doesn't expect me to know the answer
- ❏ my answer won't be good enough
- ❏ my answer will be treated with respect

Changing Perspectives in the Classroom (continued)

Two other questions to think about as if you were a student:

1. What did I learn and was it relevant? If "yes," what did I learn? If "no," does it really matter?

_____

2. If I did learn something, how will I use my learning and what would I change to make it an even better experience for me?

_____

Now, let's switch hats.

B. As teacher, consider the following questions. They may be useful in helping you to think about the environment of your classroom and to reflect on how that may affect learning.

Beginning the class:

• What kinds of behaviors do I see at the beginning of my class?

_____

• What kinds of behaviors please me and what kinds make me uncomfortable or angry or sad (or all three)?

_____

• How can I capitalize on what pleases me and how can I change what I don't much like?

_____

• How much of this behavior has to do with what I am doing or have done?

_____

• How much has to do with things beyond my control?

_____

• Are these things really beyond my control?

_____

During the class:

• What kinds of behaviors do I see?

_____

• What kinds of behaviors please me because I can see that my students are engaged with both the material and me?

_____

• What kinds of behaviors suggest to me that my students are either not with me or with the material?

_____

Changing Perspectives in the Classroom (continued)

- Students' behavior
  - ☐ Has this to do with me?
  - ☐ Has this to do with the material?
  - ☐ Has this to do with the way I am transmitting the material?
  - ☐ Has this to do with them and with their experiences over which I have no control?
  - ☐ Am I kidding myself?

- What sorts of questions am I asking?
  - ☐ Questions that always follow from easy to hard
  - ☐ Questions that offer multiple ways of thinking
  - ☐ Questions that help my students relate to what they are learning
  - ☐ Questions that can be answered with a "yes" or a "no"
  - ☐ Questions that invite students to express their feelings as well as their knowledge?
  - ☐ Questions that get in the way of the learning
  - ☐ Questions that allow students to reflect (and am I finding the time to allow it?)

Ending the class:

- What kinds of behaviors do I see?

  _____

  _____

- What signs are there that this has been a good experience for my students?

  _____

  _____

- What signs are there that this has been a good experience for me?

  _____

  _____

- What signs tell me that I will need to make more effort as a presenter? Clarify my notes (again!), relax and enjoy myself more?

  _____

  _____

For next time:

One thing to try: _____

Two things to think about: _____

_____

Thanks to Mem Fox whose suggestions for a language arts evaluation in *Radical Reflections* (1993, pp. 82, 83) served as the inspiration for this reflective exercise.

Getting Started: A Thinking Process for Teachers

These questions were designed by Margaret Burke in 2001 to help teachers think about getting started in a new classroom, a new position, or a new school. You might, from your own experience, find other questions to add to the list.

Purpose

What am I *going* to teach?
What do I *have* to teach?
What do I *want* to teach?
What do I *need* to teach to this class at this time? (Social skills? Curriculum expectations? Subject skills?)

Questions for Me to Ask Myself

What exactly do I know about *this* class?
What will I *need* to know before I begin?
How will I get that information?
What do I want *these* students at *this* time to know about the topic?
What might they already know about this topic before we start?
How can I find out where they at in relation to the topic?
What do they need to know before the unit gets going?
What exactly do I know about the topic?
What can I handle? Are there things about this topic that I would rather not deal with?

Learning Outcomes

What do I see to be the important themes?
How can I frame them as key questions or statements to guide my planning?
What are the most important learning outcomes of this curriculum unit for my students?
What other hidden curriculum learning outcomes are possible?
How well do these outcomes match?
What could be the culminating task?

Relevance

How is this topic relevant to my students as individuals and as a class?
How can I make it relevant to them?

Strategies for Action

What questions or statements will really grab the students' interest right from the start?
How can I best turn the learning into "doing something"?
Who are my teaching neighbors at this time of day? What is their noise level tolerance?

Focus

What is my focus for the overall unit?
Keeping that focus in mind, what is my focus for the introductory lesson? (Interest? Content? Reflective questions?)
What will be my reflective questions so that the students are reminded of what they have been working on or learning?
What may be my focus for the next lesson? And possibly the next? And the next? (These cannot be decided too much ahead of time, but you should have some sense of where your lessons are or might be going.)
How many lessons can I assign this topic given the aspects of the curriculum that must be covered?
How can I best sum up what we have learned?

Getting Started: A Thinking Process for Teachers (continued)

Assessment

How will I assess this material? (Personal work? Group work? How? When? More than once?)

What assessment structures will be best? (How many different kinds?)

How will the criteria be set? (Will it be by me? by the students? together?)

Realistically, are the students able to do this? (Have I given them the tools for assessing?)

Where might I look for assessment help or ideas? (Which books? Whom could I ask?)

Other things to consider:

Materials

Do I have enough back-up material?

Is it the right kind of material for the job?

Are these available? Where?

Are they available to me when I want them?

What arrangements do I have to make to ensure that they are available?

Can I get my hands on more (material, information) if or when I need it? How quickly?

Note: It is helpful to know where things are stored and how to access them. Where are such things as books, CD player, tape deck, overhead or slide projector, video equipment, PowerPoint, paper, pens, pencils, flow pens, glue, scissors, chairs, table, boxes?

How do I access the copier and how do I unlock and lock up?

Really Important Questions

Does the technical stuff all work?

What are its idiosyncrasies?

Do I have the necessary keys?

Do I need to practise using the equipment before class?

Availability

Can I rely on the material being available, or do I have to book it?

If I am booking it, how long are the teaching periods so that I may have the equipment for as long as I need it?

Space

What kind of working space do I have?

Do I have to share it? With whom?

Do they teach in the same subject area, or are they teaching different subjects?

Are there areas in the space that might be dangerous?

Note: Who shares your space will have an impact on the ways you make your classroom welcoming, post student work, and so on.

Interference

How much interference is there likely to be from the bell/buzzer intercom system or phone?

What rules apply to cellphone use in class?

What interference may I expect from staff or other students?

What is the protocol for class interruptions?

Names

What are the names of the custodians, secretaries, my peers, and the students I teach?

Getting Started: A Thinking Process for Teachers (continued)

School Policies

In order to prevent possible difficulties that might arise from the material you choose or the references you use, these questions may be helpful:

What is the nature of the district I serve?

What are the policies of the school with regard to the neighborhood in relation to culture, ethnicities, religious inclinations, established behavioral policies, and languages?

Is there anything special I should know about the school or its environs? Who could I ask?

Support

What are the phone numbers of my own particular support system (personal and professional)?

Personal Attributes

What personal skills and attributes do I bring to my teaching?

What personal as well as professional goals have I set myself?

How will I present myself to my students? (In style of speech? In what I wear?)

What sort of role model do I intend to be?

What is my attitude towards homework? Towards getting it done (students' responsibility)? Towards getting it marked and returned promptly to students (my responsibility)?

Relating to Other Staff and Administration

What are the special skills and attributes of my peers?

Do I feel able to ask for help when I need it?

Do I believe I should be self-sufficient?

How do I react to unsolicited advice?

Am I a good listener?

Do I talk too much?

Am I ready to give a hand when asked?

Bibliography

Aker, D. (1995). *Hitting the Mark: Assessment Tools for Teachers*. Markham, ON: Pembroke.

Ambrosino, Salvatore, (Ed.). (n.d.) *We, the Family: Plays for Living*. New York: Family Service Bureau.

Arnold, Roslyn. (1998). The drama in research—and articulating dynamics. In J. Saxton and C. Miller (Eds.), *The Research of Practice/The Practice of Research* (pp. 110–131). Victoria, BC: IDEA Publications.

Arts Education Research Agenda for the Future. (1994). National Endowment for the Arts/U.S. Department of Education.

Barnes, Douglas. (1976). *The Writer in Australia: A Collection of Literary Documents*. Melbourne, AU: Oxford University Press.

Benjamen, Alfred. (1981). *The Helping Interview*. Boston: Houghton Mifflin.

Berlak, Ann, and Berlak, Harold. (1987). Teachers working with teachers to transform schools. In J. Smyth (Ed.), *Educating Teachers: Changing the Nature of Pedagogical Knowledge* (pp. 169–78). Lewes: The Falmer Press.

Beyer, Landon. (1988). *Knowing and Acting: Inquiry, Ideology and Educational Studies*. London: The Falmer Press.

Bidwell, P. (1990, March). "Quescussion" workshop. St. Catharines, ON: Brock University.

Blackburn, Simon. (1988, November 20). Interview. *Sunday Observer*.

Bloom, Benjamin S., and Krathwohl, David R. (1965). *The Taxonomy of Educational Objectives, The Classification of Educational Goals*. Handbook 1: *Cognitive Domain*. New York: D. McKay.

Bolton, Gavin. (1979). *Towards a Theory of Drama in Education*. London: Longman.

Booth, Eric. (1999). *The Everyday Work of Art*. Naperville, IL: Sourcebooks.

Britton, James. (1970). *Language and Learning: The Importance of Speech in Children's Development*. London: Allen Lane.

Brooks, W., and Emmert, P. (1976). *Interpersonal Communication*. Dubuque, IO: W. C. Brown.

Brownlie, F., Close, S., and Wingren, L. (1988). *Reaching for Higher Thought*. Edmonton, AB: Arnold.

Bruner, Jerome. (1986). *Actual Minds, Possible Worlds*. Cambridge, MA: Harvard University Press.

Bruner, Jerome. (1996). *The Culture of Education*. Cambridge, MA: Harvard University Press.

Buford, B. (2006). *Heat*. Toronto: Doubleday.

Burke, Margaret. (2001). "Getting started." Unpublished teaching handout.

Cambridge, G., (Ed.). (1949). *Bacon's Essays*. London: Oxford University Press.

Carlson, M. (1998). *Performance: A Critical Introduction*. London: Routledge.

Chambers, Aidan. (1996). *Tell Me*. Portland, ME: Stenhouse.

Center for the Study of Teaching and Policy. (1998). Description and synopsis of research program. *Policy and Excellent Teaching: Focus for a National Research Center*.

Cole, A. (2002). *Better Answers: Written Performance That Looks Good and Sounds Smart*. Portland, ME: Stenhouse.

Damasio, Antonio. (1994). *Descartes' Error: Emotion, Reason, and the Human Brain*. New York: Avon Books.

Damasio, Antonio. (1999). *The Feeling of What Happens: Body and Emotion in the Making of Consciousness*. New York: Harcourt.

Davies, Robertson. (1998). *Happy Alchemy: Writings on the Theatre and Other Lively Arts*. Toronto: Penguin Books.

Davis, J. H. (2005). Redefining Ratso Rizzo: Learning from the arts about process and reflection. *Phi Delta Kappan, 87*(1), 11–17.

Deasy, Richard. (2001). Keynote. Tucson Symposium on the Arts. Tucson, AZ. February.

Deasy, Richard, (Ed.). (2002). *Critical Links: Learning in the Arts and Student Academic and Social Development*. Washington, DC: Arts Education Partnership.

Dillon, J. T. (1983). *Teaching and the Art of Questioning*. Bloomington: Phi Delta Kappa Educational Foundation.

Dillon, J. T. (1988a). *Questioning and Discussion: A Multidisciplinary Study*. Norwood, NJ: Ablex Publishing.

Dillon, J. T. (1988b). *Teaching and Questioning: A Manual of Practice*. London: Croom Helm.

Drake, S. (1998). *Creating Integrated Curriculum: Proven Ways to Increase Student Learning*. Thousand Oaks, CA: Corwin Press.

Dressel, Susan. (1981). The reference base: How to assess the students' meaning. *Phi Delta Kappan* (February), 457–458.

Dryden, Ken. (1995). *In School: Our Kids, Our Teachers, Our Classrooms*. Toronto: McClelland & Stewart.

Duncan, Ronald. (n.d.) "Ra."

Edwards, A. E., and Westgate, D. P. G. (1987). *Investigating Classroom Talk*. Social Research and Educational Series 4. London and Philadelphia: The Falmer Press.

Edwards, Derek, and Mercer, Neil. (1987). *Common Knowledge: The Development of Understanding in the Classroom*. London: Methuen.

Encyclopaedia Britannica. (1962). Feelings/Emotions. Volume 9. London: William Benton.

Egan, Kieran. (1987). *Teaching as Storytelling*. London, ON: Althouse.

Eisner, Elliot. (1994). *The Educational Imagination: On the Design and Evaluation of School Programs* (3rd ed.). New York: Macmillan.

Estes, Thomas, and Vasquez-Levy, Dorothy. (2001). Literature as a source of information and values. *Phi Delta Kappan, 82*(7), 507–512.

Ferrara, Charles L. (1981). The joys of leading a discussion. *English Journal, 70* (February), 68–71.

Fox, Mem. (1993). *Radical Reflections*. New York: Harcourt Brace & Company.

Freire, Paulo, and Faundez, Antonio. (1989). *Learning to Question: A Pedagogy of Liberation*. (T. Coates, Trans.), Geneva, SW: WCC Publications.

Frye, Northrop. (1988). *On Education*. Markham, ON: Fitzhenry & Whiteside.

Gardner, Howard. (1991). *The Unschooled Mind*. New York: Simon & Schuster.

Gardner, Howard. (1999). *The Disciplined Mind: What All Students Should Understand*. New York: Simon & Schuster.

Garrison, W. (2003). Democracy, experience, and education: Promoting a continued capacity for growth. *Phi Delta Kappan, 84*(7), 525–529.

Good, T. L., Salvings, R. L., Harel, K. H., and Emerson, H. (1987). Student passivity. *Sociology of Education, 60*, 181–199.

Grahame, Kenneth. (1908). *The Wind in the Willows*. London: Methuen.

Graves, Donald H. (1983). *Writing: Teachers and Children at Work*. Portsmouth, NH: Heinemann.

Greene, M. (2006). Poetry and patriotism. *Phi Delta Kappan, 87*(8), 596.

Hannam, Charles, Smyth, Pat, and Stephenson, Norman. (1977). *Young Teachers and Reluctant Learners* (Revised ed.). Harmondsworth, UK: Penguin Books.

Hart, N. (2002, January 29). Reflection on questioning workshop. Faculty of Education, University of Victoria.

Hawkins, T. (1976). *Group Inquiry Techniques for Teaching Writing*. Urbana, IL: National Council of Teachers of English.

Hoff, Benjamin. (1982). *The Tao of Pooh*. New York: E. P. Dutton.

Holdstock, P. (2004). *Mortal Distractions*. Saskatoon, SK: Thistledown Press.

Holt, John. (1982). *How Children Fail* (Revised ed.). New York: Dell.

Homer-Dixon, T. (2000). *The Ingenuity Gap: Can We Solve the Problems of the Future?* Toronto: Vintage Canada.

Hubbard, R., and Power, B. (1999). *Living the Questions: A Guide for Teacher-Researchers*. Portland, ME: Stenhouse Publishers.

Hughes, B. (2002, January 29). Reflection on questioning workshop. Faculty of Education, University of Victoria.

Hunkins, Francis P. (1974). *Questioning Strategies and Techniques*. Boston, MA: Allyn & Bacon.

Kahne, Joseph, and Middaugh, Ellen. (2006). Is patriotism good for democracy? A study of high school seniors' patriotic commitments. *Phi Delta Kappan, 87*(8), 600–604.

Kahne, Joseph, and Westheimer, Joel. (2003). Teaching democracy: What schools need to do. *Phi Delta Kappan, 85*(1), 34–40, 57–67.

Keefe, J., and Jenkins, J. (2002). Personalized instruction. *Phi Delta Kappan, 83*(6), 440–448.

Kelly, George. (1963). *Theory of Personality: The Psychology of Personal Constructs*. New York: Norton Library.

Kenna, Kathleen. (1988, December 8). Temagami. *Toronto Star*.

Kim, J., and Sunderman, G. (2005). Measuring academic proficiency under the No Child Left Behind Act: Implication for educational equity. *Educational Researcher, 34*(8), 3–13.

Kohn, A. (2004). Test today, privatize tomorrow: Using accountability to "reform" public schools to death. *Phi Delta Kappan, 85*(8), 568–577.

Kraft, Ulrich. (2005). Unleashing creativity. *Scientific American Mind, 16*(1), 17–21.

Kurfiss, Joanne Gainen. (1989). Critical thinking by design. *Teaching Excellence: Toward the Best in the Academy*. Autumn. Distributed by The Centre for Teaching Excellence: University of Hawaii at Manoa: 1–2.

Laidlaw, Linda. (1989). Some further thoughts on questioning. (Unpublished). Toronto.

Laidlaw, Linda. (2005). *Reinventing Curriculum: A Complex Perspective on Literacy and Writing*. Mahwah, NJ: Lawrence Erlbaum Associates.

Langer, E. (1997). *The Power of Mindful Learning*. Reading, MA: Addison-Wesley.

Laurence, Margaret. (1978). *A Bird in the House*. Toronto: McClelland & Stewart.

Lenzen, M. (2005). Perspectives: Feeling our emotions. An interview with Antonio Damasio. *Scientific American Mind, 16*(1), 14, 15.

Lewis, A. (2006). Washington commentary: Clean up the test mess. *Phi Delta Kappan, 87*(9), 643–645.

Malczewski, Carol. (1990). Towards a theory of ownership in the dramatic process. Masters thesis, University of Victoria (Unpublished).

Mankell, Henning. (2004). *The Fifth Woman*. (S. Murray, Trans.). New York: Vintage Random House.

Manzo, A. V. (1969). The ReQuest Procedure. *Journal of Reading, 13*(2), 123–126.

Marshall, Richard, (Ed.). (1977). *Great Events of the Twentieth Century*. Montreal: Reader's Digest Association.

Maslow, Abraham. (1968). *Towards a Psychology of Being*. New York: Van Nostrand.

Mason, G. (2006, May 20). School rankings flawed but useful. *The Globe and Mail*, p. S1.

Mayes, F. (1996). *Under the Tuscan Sun*. New York: Broadway Books.

McKeachie, W. J. (1978). *Starting Discussion with a Question: Teaching Tips: A Guidebook for the Beginning College Teacher*. Washington, DC: D. C. Heath.

McTeague, R. (1992). *Shared Reading in the Middle and High School Years*. Portsmouth, NH: Heinemann.

Meier, Deborah. (2002). Standardization versus standards. *Phi Delta Kappan, 8*(3), 190–198.

Meier, Deborah. (2003). So what does it take to build a school for democracy? *Phi Delta Kappan, 85*(1), 15–21.

Michener, James A. (1987). *Legacy*. New York: Fawcett Crest.

Miller, Arthur. (1965). *The Crucible*. New York: Viking.

Miller, C., and Saxton, Juliana. (2004a). Standards: The illusion of comfort. *Arts Praxis*, 1, 38–42. http://www.nyu.edu/education/music/artspraxis.

Miller, C., and Saxton, Juliana. (2004b). *Into the Story: Language in Action through Drama*. Portsmouth, NH: Heinemann.

Moffett, James, and Wagner, Betty Jane. (1976). *Student-Centered Language Arts and Reading, K–13: A Handbook for Teachers*. Boston: Houghton Mifflin.

Moore, Kathleen, and McEwen, Jessie. (1936). *A Picture History of Canada*. Toronto: Nelson.

Morgan, Norah, and Saxton, Juliana. (1987). *Teaching Drama: A Mind of Many Wonders*. London: Hutchinson.

Morgan, Norah, and Saxton, Juliana. (1989, May). Not asked for. In OISE, *Forum for the Arts and Media Education*, Toronto.

Murphy, J. (2006). An interview with Henry Mintzberg. *Phi Delta Kappan, 87*(7), 527, 528.

National Survey of Student Engagement. (2004). Retrieved 5 May 2006. Available at http://www.pair.ubc.ca/studies/Summary%20NSSE%202004.pdf.

Neelands, Jonothan. (1990). *Structuring Drama Work*. Cambridge, UK: Cambridge University Press.

Noddings, Nel. (2004). War, critical thinking and self-understanding. *Phi Delta Kappan, 85*(7), 489–495.

Norman, John. (1987, September). Notes taken from a workshop at the British Council course "How do you train a drama teacher?" Stanhope, 6–18.

Nunan, D., and Lamb, C. (1996). *The Self-Directed Theatre: Managing the Learning Process*. Cambridge, UK: Cambridge University Press.

O'Neill, Cecily, and Lambert, Alan. (1982). *Drama Structures: A Handbook for Teachers*. London: Hutchinson.

Ontario Ministry of Education. (1988). *Science Is Happening Here*. Policy statement for science in Primary and Junior Divisions.

O'Sullivan, C. (1998). (Re)Laying the foundations for a child-centred curriculum in Drama and Education. In C. O'Sullivan and G. Williams (Eds.), *Building Bridges: Laying the Foundations for Child-Centred Curriculum in Drama and Education* (pp. 158–178). Birmingham, UK: NATD Press.

Patterson, William. (2003). Breaking out of our boxes. *Phi Delta Kappan, 84*(8), 569–574.

Pearce, T. (2006, January 14). Wired up, plugged in, zoned out. *The Globe and Mail*, F8.

Pinker, S. (1997). *How the Mind Works*. New York: W. W. Norton.

Postman, Neil. (1979). *Teaching as a Conserving Activity*. New York: Dell.

Postman, Neil, and Weingartner, Charles. (1969). *Teaching as a Subversive Activity*. New York: Delacorte.

Primary English Notes. (n.d.). Why ask? Your guide to good questioning. *Primary Teaching Notes* No. 10, prepared by Bruce Cornish (R. D. Walshe, ed.). Australia: Primary English Teaching Association of New South Wales.

Purkey, William. (1978). *Inviting School Success: A Self-Concept Approach to Teaching and Learning*. Belmont, CA: Wadsworth.

Rallis, S., Tedder, J., Lachman, A., and Elmore, R. (2006). Superintendents in classrooms: From collegial conversation to collaborative action. *Phi Delta Kappan, 87*(7), 537–545.

Robertson, H-J. (1998). *No More Teachers, No More Books: The Commercialization of Canada's Schools*. Toronto: McClelland & Stewart.

Romanow, Roy. (2006). A house half built. *The Walrus, 3*(5), 48–54.

Roth, Jason. (n.d.). *Why Can't You Hear What I Haven't Said?: A Compilation of Writings and Thoughts on Creative Listening and Communication*. Halifax, NS.

Rundle, L. (2005). Portrait of a master. *University of Toronto Alumni Magazine*. (Summer), 17.

Sanders, M. (2002). *From Here You Can't See Paris: Seasons of a French Village and Its Restaurants*. New York: Harper Collins.

Saul, John Ralston. (1993). *Voltaire's Bastards: The Dictatorship of Reason in the West*. Toronto: Viking/Penguin.

Saul, John Ralston. (1995). *The Unconscious Civilization*. Concord, ON: House of Anansi Press.

Saxton, Juliana, and Verriour, Patrick. (1988). A sense of ownership. (National Association of Drama in Education, Australia) *NADIE Journal, 12*(2), 9–12.

Schaffner, Megan. (1983). *The Power of Drama: A Case Study of Drama in a Primary School*. Tasmania, AU: Speech and Drama Centre.

Shortz, W. (2001, April 8). How to solve the New York Times Crossword puzzle. New York: New York Times Company. n.p.

Stewart, R., and Brendfur, J. (2005). Fusing lesson study and authentic achievement: A model for teacher collaboration. *Phi Delta Kappan, 86*(9), 681–687.

Stoppard, Tom. (1967). *Rosencrantz and Guildenstern Are Dead*. London: Samuel French.

Taylor, P. (1996). Reflective practitioner research. In B. J. Wagner (Ed.), *Educational Drama and Language Arts: What the Research Shows* (pp. 212–230). Portsmouth, NH: Heinemann.

Tizard, B., and Hughes, M. (1984). *Young Children Learning: Talking and Thinking at Home and School*. London: Fontana.

University of Alabama School of Medicine, Office of Curriculum Development & Management. (n.d.). *Teaching Tips: Effective Questioning*. Retrieved 29 January 2006. Available at http://www.uab.edu/uasomume/cdm/questioning.htm#Techniques.

Van Manen, M. (1992). *Researching Lived Experience: Human Science for an Action Sensitive Pedagogy*. London, ON: Althouse Press.

Vygotsky, Lev. (1986). *Thought and Language* (Revised ed.). Boston: MIT Press.

Wagner, Betty Jane. (1998). *Educational Drama and Language Arts: What the Research Shows*. Portsmouth, NH: Heinemann.

Watson, P. (1998, April 18). Forget your troubles. C'mon get happy. *The Globe and Mail*. E1.

Weingartner, Charles. (1977). Remedial reasoning. National Council of Teachers of English, *English Journal* (May), 12–14.

Windschitl, M. (2002). Framing constructivism in practice as the negotiation of dilemmas: An analysis of the conceptual, pedagogical, cultural and political challenges facing teachers. *Review of Educational Research 72*(2), 121–176.

Woods, P. (1987). Life histories and teacher knowledge. In J. Smyth (Ed.), *Educating Teachers: Changing the Nature of Pedagogical Knowledge* (pp. 121–135). Lewes: The Falmer Press.

Zull, James E. (2002). *The Art of Changing the Brain: Enriching the Practice of Teaching by Exploring the Biology of Learning*. Sterling, VA: Stylus.

Index

Active listeners 78
Active responding process 78–79
Active silence 78
Affective domain 15, 16
Analysis 19, 22–23, 25, 63
Answers
    Choral 95–96
    Dealing with 91–93
    No 93
    Responding to 93–98
    Wrong 93
Application 19, 22, 64

Bloom's taxonomy 18, 34, 44, 63, 64
Body gestures 88
Body language 88–89
Body position 89
Building questions upon questions
    Response form 135
    Teacher's notes 134

Changing perspectives in the classroom 142–144
Characteristics of a citizen 15
Choral answers 95–96
Classroom discourse 74–75, 82, 93, 130
    Characteristics of effective 75–77
    Enabling 76
Classroom environment pressure 100, 103
Classroom interaction 74
Cognition 17
Cognitive domain 15
Committing 28, 29, 33
Comprehension 19, 21–22, 64
Compromise 10
Control pressure 100, 103–104
Curriculum pressure 100, 102–103

Dealing with answers 91–93
Democracy 9, 11, 128
Dialogue 17
Discussion 130
    Conducting 131
    Model for 131

Educational process 15–16
Effective learning 17, 27, 74
Effective teaching 17, 27, 31
Emotional engagement 27
Emotions 29
Empathy 10

Encouraging 108
Engaging 28, 29, 33
Evaluating 28, 31, 33
Evaluating questions on Ann Graham
    Response form 140
    Teacher's notes 139
Evaluation 19, 24, 25, 63
Example lesson
    Ann Graham 119–128, 139–140
    Finding areas 55–62
    Snow White 34–44
Eye contact 88

Facial expression 88, 94
Feelings 29
Focusing 109
Functions 73

General teaching requirements 82–83
    Classroom arrangement 82
    Classroom conduct 82
    Lesson focus and objective 82–83
    Observation 83
    Voice and intonation 83
General teaching techniques 83–85
    Deal with response that downgrades contribution 85
    Elevate language 84
    Give an answer weight 84
    Give opportunities for rethinking and restating 85
    Universalize the answer 84
    Use clear, direct language 83
Getting started: Thinking process for teachers 145–147

Habits of mind 10
Hand over 33
Hidden curriculum 10

Interest 28, 33
    Aggressive 28
    Passive 28
Internalizing 28, 29–30, 33
Interpreting 28, 30, 33

Knowledge 19, 64

Modelling how to question 107, 108–109
    Covert 107
    Overt 108–109

Negotiation 10, 27

Objectivity 11
Organization 74
Ownership through deepening engagement 31

Participation 9, 16, 17, 87
Partners in dialogue 99
Personal dispositions 10
Personal pressure 100–101
Praising 108
Pressure
    Addressing 100–105
    Classroom environment 100, 103
    Classroom teacher 100
    Control 100, 103–104
    Curriculum 100, 102–103
    Personal 100–101
    Right-answer 100, 101–102
    Standardized testing 100, 104–105
Pressures on classroom teachers 100
    Addressing 100–105
Probing 89–90
    Counselling 90
Process 46
Process of inquiry 99
Process of ownership 31
Promoting responsibility for learning 105–106
Psychomotor domain 15

Question recitation 81
Questioning 11, 74, 100
    Asking 109
    Art of 78, 80
    Better 11
    Building a story through 122–126
    Distorting the place of 18
    Effective 12, 13, 14, 17, 63, 76–77, 82
    Good 15, 78
    Language art 13
    Responsibility for 99
    Role of taxonomy 31–33
    Role play 116
    Some roles that promote 117
    Study guide 113
    Training and practice in 109–118
Questioning behaviors 141
Questioning skills 11, 106
    Addressing the pressures against teaching of
        100–105
    Development 118
    Effective 128
    Promoting student 119
Questions
    Abstract 86
    Alternatives to 72–73
    Ambiguous 69–70, 77

Analysing 110, 118, 127
Appropriate 111
Asking 9, 13, 83, 101
Assessing and recording 12
Branching 65
Building questions upon 134, 135
Category A 45, 46–48, 54, 73, 139
Category B 45, 46, 48–51, 54, 73, 92, 139
Category C 45, 46, 51–54, 73, 92, 139
Clarifying 68
Classification by general function 45–46
Classification of 45–54, 73
Closed 64, 114
Complex 24, 86
Comprehension 45
Confrontation 65
Contrapuntal 70
Convergent 18
Correspondence with answers 75
Counter 96
Covert 63, 64
Covert ways to model 107
Creating 23
Creative 66
Critical 65
Deductive 65, 66
Demanding inference and interpretation 50–51
Developing critical assessment or value judgments
    53–54
Developing suppositions or hypotheses 52
Development 68
Different forms of 110
Difficult 128
Directing 85–87
Discovering what they do 110
Distribution of 85–87
Divergent 18, 63, 66–67
Double-barrelled 70
Drawing upon knowledge 20–21
Driving 65
Educative 66
Effective 13–14, 17
Elicitation 70
Eliciting information 45, 46–48, 73
Enactive 67
Encouraging analysis 22–23
Essential 71
Establishing or helping control group discipline 47
Establishing or helping control procedure 47
Establishing procedure 47
Establishing rules of the game 46–47
Eternal 71
Evaluating 68
Everyday 71
Examining how they helped build the story 127–128

Factual 67, 86
Flexible, non-hierarchical use of 54
Focusing on future action or projection 52–53
Focusing on making connections 49
Focusing on meanings behind textual context 51
Focusing on personal feelings 52
Focusing on recall of facts 48
Following 68
Freeing 66
General functions 11
Glossary 63–73
Good 13–14, 15, 74, 77–78, 80, 91
Hard 128
Heuristic 66
Higher-order 63
How to use taxonomy to help frame 33
Hypothetical 66
Implied 68
Inductive 65, 66
Inviting synthesis 23
Judging 24
Key 63, 65, 83
Leading 69, 79, 97
Loaded 69
Lower-order 64
Machine-gun 69
Making up test 113
Marathon 69
Mirror 68
Open 64
Opening 67–68
Overt 64
Overt ways to model 108–109
Polar 65
Pressing for reflection 45, 46, 51–54, 73
Pressing students to rethink or restate 49
Principles 46
Probing 67, 89–90
Problems with distributing 86
Process 68
Productive 11, 13, 66
Promoting evaluation 24
Promoting expression of attitudes, biases and points
   of view 50
Prompt 70
Purpose of 44, 110
Raising 119–121, 128
Reasoning 22–23
Recall 18, 67
Reflective 67
Remembering 20–21
Rephrasing 127
Requiring a written reply 66
Requiring application 22
Revealing experience 48

Review 68
Rhetorical 67
Right-answer 97
Serialized 69
Shaping understanding 45, 46, 48–51, 73
Silly 68
Simple 18, 24
Social 67
Solving 22
Starter 114
Student 100, 101
Stupid 69
Summary 68
Supplying information and suggesting implications
   48
Synopsis 68
Synthesizing 23, 24
Targeting 85–87
Testing comprehension 21–22
Thick 75
Thin 75
Thinker 67
Tough 65
Twenty 114
Unanswerable 71
Understanding 21–22
Unifying class 47
Value of 14
Valuing 127
When not to ask 90–91
Who asks 132, 133
Why 70–71
Why aren't more coming from students 100
Why teachers ask so many 79–80

Rationality 11
Recitation 71
   Question 81
Reflecting/Analysing 108–109
Reflection 46, 105
Reflective restatements 72
Reinforcement 87–89
   Minimal 88
   Non-verbal 88–89, 94
   Verbal 87–88
ReQuest procedure 112
Responding to answers
   What to avoid 93–98
Responsibilities 9
Right-answer pressure 100, 101–102
Rights of the citizen 10
Role playing 116–118
   Grouping 117

Scaffolding 76

Sequential progression 31
Side chat 85
Social talk 130
Standardized testing pressure 100, 104–105
Statements 72–73
    Declarative 72
    Invitational 73
    State of mind 72
Structure for feeling 11
Structure for thinking 11
Student as questioner
    Case for 99–106
    Switching places 107–118
Synthesis 19, 23, 25, 63

Tapping in 125
Taxonomy 31
    Bloom's 18, 34, 44, 63, 64
    Educational objectives 19
    Knowing 44
    Personal engagement 27–28, 33, 62
    Reflections on the use of 44
Taxonomy of educational objectives 19
Taxonomy of personal engagement 27–28, 33, 62
Thinking
    Kinds of 20–24, 46
    Quality time 78
    Question of 18–26
    Synonyms 19
Thinking aloud 108
Thinking as someone else
    Response form 137–138
    Teacher's notes 136
Thinking skills 21, 22, 23, 24
Thinking time 80–81
Thoughtful answers 79
Thoughtful learning environment 87
Training and practice in questioning 109–118
    Analysing a tape-recording 118
    Answer/Question 115–116
    Building the rules 109–110
    Conducting an inquiry/Working scientifically
      111–112

Discovering what questions do 110
Hot seating 114–115
Making up test questions 113
Question/Question 115
ReQuest procedure 112
Role-playing 116–118
Some roles that promote questioning 117
Study guide questioning 113
Twenty questions 114
Transfer 33

Vigorous learner 16–17

Wait time 80
What to avoid when responding to answers 93–98
    Answering your own questions 96
    Asking another question before student contributes 96
    Asking for choral answers 95–96
    Asking questions that have been answered 96
    Asking questions that students cannot answer 95
    Asking questions too soon 98
    Asking questions when students are too tired to think 98
    Collecting answers until you get the one you want 97
    Counter-questioning 96
    Hearing only what you want to hear 98
    Insincere praise 98
    Manipulating responses by non-verbal signals 94
    Phrasing the question for the answer you want 97
    Reacting to every contribution 94–95
    Redirecting a right-answer question 97
    Reinforcing prejudices 95
    Responding with "Yes, but" or "Yes, and" 94
    Verbal responses that are detrimental to learning 94
Who asks questions
    Response form 133
    Teacher's notes 132
Writing based on information gathered 126

Postscript

Norah Morgan, D.Litt. (Hon.)

to harness: from the Old English *gaed*, meaning fellowship

team: from Old Frisian *tam*, meaning bridle

Norah and I were delighted to be asked to think about a second edition and were at work on revisions, emendations, corrections (always needed, however carefully edited!) and new ideas. Our schedule, however, was interrupted by her death. A thoughtful person as well as a veteran of the Second World War (having served in the WAF as a radar officer), Norah chose to leave us on November 11, 2004, a day that makes it possible always to remember and to celebrate her life. Not that those of us who knew her would ever forget her. To her friends, she was loyal, generous, hospitable, and full of the sheer joy of living; to her students, colleagues, and scholars (local, national, and international), she was a teacher and drama educator of inestimable worth. To me, she was all those things and more.

In 1998, we were invited to contribute to a book on collaboration. After much thought, we declined. We felt that talking about how we worked together would inhibit the whole process (much like actors who never want to watch what they are doing). I remember once, when we were working on our first book, we decided to use a tape recorder to capture all those splendid insights. I set it up. We sat . . . and sat . . . and sat. Then Norah said: "Oh, turn the damn thing off. I can't think of a thing to say with it sitting there waiting!" All we could offer in response to that invitation was that "ever since we met, whenever we work in the kitchen, we never bump into each other." Perhaps it was this kinesthetic intelligence that lay at the heart of our collaboration—physical and mental. When we were harnessed together as a team, we respected each other's space; adapted our rhythms; recognized that when the ground was uneven, it made different demands upon each of us; and knew that there was nothing more satisfying and enjoyable than when we were pulling together and that it was the journey that mattered to us.

Norah was always concerned about the "foo-foo," a neat phrase that she invented to describe the impenetrable academese that we often came across in the process of research. It was a phrase that she also used about my more extravagant forays into our writing. Happily, together we had accomplished quite a bit of this revision before her death. Required to complete this second edition on my own, I have tried to maintain her clarity of expression, passion for practical illustrations drawn from classroom practice, and joy in the work.

Juliana Saxton, Victoria, B.C., 2006